# 200
## VEGETARIAN
## STUDENT MEALS

# HAMLYN **ALL COLOUR COOKBOOKS**

To view the complete list of
Hamlyn All Colour titles visit
www.octopusbooks.co.uk

THE WORLD'S MOST TRUSTED COOKBOOKS
OVER **15 MILLION** COPIES SOLD

# 200

HAMLYN **ALL COLOUR COOKBOOK**

## VEGETARIAN
## STUDENT MEALS

hamlyn

# hamlyn

First published in Great Britain in 2024 by Hamlyn,
an imprint of Octopus Publishing Group Ltd
Carmelite House
50 Victoria Embankment
London EC4Y 0DZ
www.octopusbooks.co.uk

An Hachette UK Company
www.hachette.co.uk

This material was previously published in *365 Student Vegetarian Cookbook*, *Hamlyn QuickCook Budget Meals*, *Hamlyn QuickCook Family Meals* and *Hamlyn QuickCook Cakes & Bakes*.

ISBN 978-0-600-63848-3

A CIP catalogue record for this book is available from the British Library.

Printed and bound in China.
10 9 8 7 6 5 4 3 2 1

Standard level spoon measurement are used in all recipes.
1 tablespoon = one 15 ml spoon
1 teaspoon = one 5 ml spoon

Both imperial and metric measurements have been given in all recipes. Use one set of measurements only and not a mixture of both.

Eggs should be medium unless otherwise stated. The Department of Health advises that eggs should not be consumed raw. This book contains dishes made with raw or lightly cooked eggs. It is prudent for more vulnerable people such as pregnant and nursing mothers, the elderly, babies and young children to avoid uncooked or lightly cooked dishes made with eggs. Once prepared these dishes should be kept refrigerated and used promptly.

Milk should be full fat unless otherwise stated.

Fresh herbs should be used unless otherwise stated. If unavailable use dried herbs as an alternative but halve the quantities stated.

Pepper should be freshly ground black pepper unless otherwise stated.

This book includes dishes made with nuts and nut derivatives. It is advisable for those with known allergic reactions to nuts and nut derivatives and those who may be potentially vulnerable to these allergies to avoid dishes made with nuts and nut oils. It is also prudent to check the labels of pre-prepared ingredients for the possible inclusion of nut derivatives.

Vegetarians should look for the 'V' symbol on a cheese to ensure it is made with vegetarian rennet.

# contents

# introduction

# introduction

Moving away to study for a degree is a huge lifestyle shift – you are likely fending for yourself for the first time, living with others outside of your family and managing your own food and house budgets.

Whether you regularly prepare food at home or are completely new to cooking, here you will find plenty of inspiration to rustle up some delicious meals that won't break the bank. A bit of planning upfront can help your budget stretch further and allow you to get a bit more creative in the kitchen.

This book has a vegetarian focus and the great thing about eating vegetarian on a student budget is that fresh fruit and vegetables are affordable, healthy and delicious, allowing you to eat well while staying within your means.

This section includes tips and tricks for eating well while living independently, from choosing the right equipment and stocking your storecupboard to managing in a communal kitchen. So, let's get started!

## Eating on a budget

Boring as it may be, budgeting is a necessary part of student life. Make sure to account for all your outgoings when working out your spending, including rent, bills, travel, food and fun. One of the benefits of planning your own home-cooked meals is it can help your money stretch further than if you were to buy the ready-made equivalent.

Another way to save might be to organize a shared food budget with your housemates. If you are the only vegetarian in your household, then it might be simpler to keep most of your budget separate, but you could at least have a shared kitty for basics like milk, bread and other household necessities. Then you could take advantage of multi-buy offers or buy larger sizes, which tend to be more cost effective (though always make sure to compare prices before buying).

For any food for yourself, not to be shared, you should agree a system with your household to help prevent your favourite cheese from disappearing out of the communal fridge! Accidents will happen, of course, but it's useful to have rules upfront of what you are sharing and what is off-limits.

## Essential kit

Student kitchens tend to have limited space, which only allows for basic cooking utensils, but you really don't need fancy gadgets to make a tasty meal.

If you know or are already in contact with your housemates, it may be a good idea to agree on what you need for the kitchen and divide it up between you. Otherwise, you'll find yourself with multiple sets of pans, plates and cutlery, which will take up unnecessary space in your kitchen.

For what you do purchase, feel free to go for a basic set and look out for deals.

Large supermarkets and department stores have a wide variety of equipment to choose from and you may even be able to get some of it second hand, either from charity shops, online or from family and friends.

Here's a list of some of the basics that will cover you for most of your cooking needs:

- Chopping board
- One small and one large kitchen knife
- Vegetable peeler
- Measuring spoons
- Can opener
- Bottle opener
- Small potato masher
- Balloon whisk
- Rolling pin
- Grater, ideally with a container below so you can grate more than you need at once
- Wooden spoon
- Spatula
- Slotted spoon
- Large metal strainer or colander
- Measuring jug
- Couple of mixing bowls that stack one inside the other
- Nonstick frying pan, preferably with a lid
- One small and one large nonstick saucepan with metal handles and lids for on the hob and in the oven
- Couple of baking sheets
- Roasting tin
- Large rectangular ovenproof dish
- Food storage containers, for lunches and storing leftovers in the fridge

A stick blender is ideal for blending soups or making smoothies, but if there's a spare food processor hanging around in a cupboard at the family home, this would be a good addition to your kitchen. They're great for chopping large quantities of vegetables, making sauces and cakes. If you want to make fresh juice and don't have a juicer, they can also be used to juice fresh fruit.

A wok and a steamer are also handy to have but not essential. You can get by with a large frying pan for stir-fries and a metal strainer or colander over a pan will work fine for steaming.

If you are interested in baking in your new student home, you might also want to consider bringing cake tins, muffin tins, pastry cutters and wire cooling racks.

## 7 cooking terms you should know

**Stir-fry:** To cook foods in a little oil in a wok or large frying pan over a high heat for just a matter of minutes, stirring all the time for even cooking.

**Shallow-fry:** To fry foods in a frying pan with 1–2 tablespoons oil.

**Steam:** To cook foods in a covered perforated saucepan set over a lower saucepan half-filled with boiling water, so it is not in direct contact with the water.

**Simmer:** To cook over a low heat so the bubbles break the surface.

**Mash:** This can be done with a fork, for example when mashing a banana or avocado on a plate until smooth. Larger amounts of vegetables are best mashed with a large metal masher or handheld stick blender.

**Roux:** This is the base of a cheese or white sauce. To make a roux, melt butter in a saucepan, then stir in flour until the mixture binds together. Cook briefly, then stir in milk with a wooden spoon until smooth. Continue to stir until the sauce comes to the boil, is a pouring thickness and hopefully lump free. If there are lumps in your sauce, these can be whisked out with a small balloon whisk.

**Creaming:** This term is used when making cakes. Butter or soft margarine is beaten with sugar in a bowl with a wooden spoon or electric mixer, if you have one, until it is creamy smooth and pale in colour.

### Getting used to your oven
All ovens vary slightly and fan ovens tend to cook food quicker than conventional ovens. The oven temperatures in this book are based on a conventional oven, so as a general rule, you should adjust the oven temperature to 10–20°C (25°F) below the temperatures given in the recipes if you are using a fan oven. Check on your food in the oven 10–15 minutes before the end of the cooking time to make sure it isn't overcooking. If your food is getting too brown but still needs more time in the oven, you can always cover the top with foil to stop it burning.

## Food safety

You might decide to cook one meal together as a household, but dinner time in a student household is often a dance of multiple people trying to cook individual meals. This can quickly lead to a mountain of washing up and kitchen counters covered in dirt and debris, which is the perfect breeding ground for bacteria.

A clean kitchen is important for your health but also makes cooking a more relaxed and enjoyable experience. With a little bit of effort each day to wash up and wipe the kitchen surfaces, you can keep on top of your kitchen, avoid any nasty bugs and avoid annoying your

other housemates! Speaking of which, why not agree a cleaning rota to make sure everyone gets involved in keeping the communal areas clean?

You also need to take care when handling and preparing food. This is easier for vegetarians, as the main culprits for food poisoning are cross-contamination with raw meat and undercooking meat; however, there are still some key points for non-meat eaters to consider:

- Rinse your fruit and vegetables thoroughly
- Eat food by its use-by date
- If food smells funky, then throw it away – it's better to be safe than sorry
- Always keep food covered
- Keep dairy and meat items, as well as raw and cooked meat, separate in the fridge (and share this guidance with any meat-eaters using the same fridge as you)
- Cook frozen fruit and vegetables from frozen
- Do not put defrosted food back in the freezer
- Only reheat food once and make sure that it is piping hot throughout after stirring. If you only need one portion reheated out of a larger dish, take out your individual portion for reheating and put the rest back in the fridge
- Don't overfill your trash and recycling bins and empty them when they're full

## The vegetarian diet

The key to a well-balanced vegetarian diet is simple: eat plenty of wholegrains (such as brown rice, barley, corn, oats and buckwheat), foods that are made from wholegrains (such as wholemeal breads, pastas and cereals), protein-rich pulses, lentils, nuts and eggs, and fresh fruit and vegetables.

Dairy products (such as butter, cheese, milk and yogurt) or non-dairy alternatives should form a smaller part of the diet. Complex carbohydrates are essential for a good diet and vital for energy (such as wholemeal bread, wholewheat pasta, brown rice, barley, corn, dried beans and bananas). Dietary fibre allows the energy from the natural sugars they contain to be released slowly, as opposed to refined sugars, which are released quickly and can leave energy levels depleted.

A healthy vegetarian diet will be high in fibre which is vital for moving the food in the bowel, helping to prevent intestinal problems and reducing the risk of bowel cancer. Foods rich in fibre can help to lower blood cholesterol, therefore it is advisable to include in most meals (such as beans and peas, cabbage, broccoli, Brussels sprouts, oats and wholegrain wheat).

Protein is essential for tissue repair and cell growth and reproduction. However, we do not need large amounts of protein in our diet and it is perfectly possible to consume the recommended amounts of protein from non-animal foods. Good sources of vegetarian protein include nuts and seeds, pulses, soya products, peas, beans, chickpeas and lentils.

## Key ingredients

The secret to being able to cook speedy meals lies in your store cupboard being well stocked with ingredients that you can use on a day-to-day basis. Remember to check on your stocks regularly and to keep topping them up.

**Store Cupboard Staples**
- Tea, coffee and/or hot chocolate
- Good-quality olive oil
- Salt and pepper
- Dried pasta and rice
- Quick-cooking pulses, such as split red lentils and yellow split peas
- Canned pulses and beans, such as kidney beans, chickpeas and cannellini beans
- Nuts and seeds, such as sunflower seeds, sesame seeds, cashew nuts, almonds and walnuts
- Soy sauce
- Honey
- Sugar
- Plain flour
- Vegetable stock
- Canned tomatoes and passata
- Tomato purée
- Dried herbs, such as basil, thyme, oregano and rosemary
- Whole spices, such as cumin seeds, coriander seeds and cinnamon sticks
- Ground spices, such as cumin, chilli powder, paprika and turmeric

You don't need a huge variety of herbs and spices but a nice selection will add a delicious depth of flavour to your dishes. Flick through the recipes and figure out which ones to start off with based on what you fancy cooking.

Keeping your fridge well stocked will enable you to put together healthy and tasty vegetarian meals in minutes. The key is to buy fresh regularly, and to only buy what you know you will use. Buy fruit and vegetables that are in season and, if possible, locally grown.

**Fresh Favourites**
- Butter
- Milk
- Cheese
- Eggs
- Bread
- Yogurt
- Lemons
- Limes
- Red chillies
- Onions
- Garlic
- Ginger
- Seasonal fruit and vegetables

Depending on your freezer space, it's a good idea to keep a spare loaf of sliced bread for emergency breakfasts. A few bags of frozen vegetables could also get you out of a tight spot, while gluts of seasonal fruit like blackberries or raspberries can be frozen and used in smoothies and desserts.

# Crowd pleasers

Need to save some money but fancy a treat? Here are some easy meals and snacks that can be made quickly and cheaply. They are all easy to scale up and can be enjoyed with friends.

### 1. Garlic bread

Heat a ridged griddle pan or frying pan until hot, add thick slices of sourdough bread and cook for 2 minutes on each side until lightly charred. Rub each bread slice with a peeled garlic clove and drizzle with extra virgin olive oil.

### 2. Guacamole

Place a halved, stoned, peeled and diced avocado in a food processor or blender with a crushed garlic clove, 1 seeded and chopped red chilli, juice of a lime, some chopped fresh coriander, and salt and pepper to taste. Process until fairly smooth and transfer to a bowl. Stir in a finely chopped, deseeded tomato and serve.

### 3. Tortilla wedges

Cut large flour tortillas into 12 wedges. Spray with olive oil spray and season one side with salt, pepper and a little cayenne pepper. Lay on a grill rack, spice-side up, and toast under a preheated medium grill for 1–2 minutes until the tortillas are crisp.

### 4. Avocado, blue cheese & spinach melt

Split a flat roll in half and spread the base with a little butter. Mash together a halved, stoned, peeled and sliced avocado, some crumbled blue cheese and a little double cream. Spread onto the base of the roll and add a few baby spinach leaves. Top and cook in a dry, hot frying pan for 4 minutes on each side or until golden and the cheese has melted.

### 5. Hummus

Place a can of chickpeas, drained, a crushed garlic clove, a glug of extra-virgin olive oil, some lemon juice, and salt and pepper to taste in a food processor or blender and process until smooth. Serve with some sticks of carrot and cucumber.

# snacks & light bites

# swiss cheese melts

Serves **4**
Preparation time **15 minutes**
Cooking time **3–4 minutes**

1 **baguette**
200 g (7 oz) **vegetarian Swiss cheese**, such as an **Emmental** or **Gruyère**, grated
1 tablespoon **wholegrain mustard**
2 tablespoons **mayonnaise**
2 **tomatoes**, deseeded and chopped
pinch of **black pepper**
1 **round lettuce**, to serve (optional)

**Cut** the baguette in half, then slice each half horizontally to form 4 long pieces.

**Place** the grated cheese in a bowl with the remaining ingredients and mix well to combine.

**Spoon** the topping over the cut side of each piece of bread and place on a baking sheet. Cook under a preheated hot grill for 3–4 minutes, until golden and bubbling. Serve hot with lettuce leaves, if desired.

**For swiss cheese pasta sauce**, slice 1 large onion and fry gently in 2 tablespoons vegetable oil for 6–7 minutes, until soft and golden. Stir in 1 tablespoon wholegrain mustard, 2 tomatoes, deseeded and chopped, 275 ml (9 fl oz) double cream and 200 g (7 oz) grated vegetarian Swiss cheese. Season well with salt and pepper, then stir over a gentle heat until the cheese has melted. Serve over cooked pasta, accompanied by a crusty baguette.

# grilled sweetcorn cobettes with herb & chilli butter

Serves **4**
Preparation time **10 minutes**
Cooking time **4−5 minutes**

4 **sweetcorn** cobs

**Herb & chilli butter**
200 g (7 oz) **butter**, softened
20 g (¾ oz) **dill**, finely
  chopped
2 **red chillies**, deseeded and
  finely chopped

**Mix** together all the ingredients for the herb and chilli butter and set aside.

**Cut** each corn cob into 3 equal-sized cobettes. Insert a wooden or metal skewer into the side of each cobette and place on a barbecue or on a hot griddle pan and cook, turning frequently, for 4−5 minutes or until lightly charred and blistered in places.

**Remove** the cobettes from the heat, brush with the butter and serve immediately.

**For sweetcorn & herb frittata**, lightly beat 6 eggs in a bowl, season and add 2 tablespoons each of chopped coriander, dill and mint. Heat 2 tablespoons olive oil in a medium, nonstick frying pan and add ½ small chopped onion, 1 deseeded and finely chopped red chilli and 2 crushed garlic cloves. Stir-fry for 3−4 minutes and then toss in 400 g (13 oz) fresh sweetcorn kernels and stir-fry for a further 2−3 minutes. Pour over the egg mixture and cook over a medium heat for 10 minutes or until the base is set. Place the frying pan under a preheated medium grill for 4−5 minutes or until the top is set and golden. Remove from the heat, cut into wedges and serve.

# deluxe eggs florentine

Serves **4**
Preparation time **10 minutes**
Cooking time **15 minutes**

12 **asparagus spears**,
  trimmed
2 tablespoons **butter**, plus
  extra for buttering
150 g (5 oz) **baby spinach**
pinch of freshly grated **nutmeg**
2 **English muffins**
1 tablespoon **vinegar**
4 large **eggs**
125 g (4 oz) **ready-made**
  **hollandaise sauce**, to serve
**salt** and **pepper**

**Blanch** the asparagus spears in a pan of boiling water for 2–3 minutes, drain and keep warm.

**Meanwhile**, melt the butter in a large frying pan, add the spinach and stir-fry for 3 minutes or until just wilted. Season with grated nutmeg, salt and black pepper.

**Split**, toast and butter the muffins.

**Poach** the eggs by bringing a saucepan of lightly salted water to the boil. Add the vinegar and reduce to a gentle simmer. Swirl the water with a fork and crack 2 of the eggs into the water. Cook for 3–4 minutes, remove carefully with a slotted spoon and repeat with the remaining 2 eggs.

**Meanwhile**, heat up the hollandaise sauce.

**Top** the toasted muffins with some spinach and a poached egg and spoon over the hollandaise. Add black pepper and serve 3 asparagus spears on the side of each.

**For spinach, asparagus & egg tortilla**, beat 6 eggs together with 12 torn basil leaves and season well. Heat 2 tablespoons olive oil in a large frying pan and add the egg mixture. Roughly chop a large handful of baby spinach leaves, 12 asparagus spears and 1 tomato. Scatter the spinach, asparagus and tomatoes evenly over the egg. Cook the tortilla for 6–8 minutes without stirring and then place under a preheated medium grill for 3–4 minutes or until golden brown all over. Cut the tortilla into wedges and serve with a green salad.

# stuffed aubergine & yogurt rolls

Serves **4**
Preparation time **20 minutes**
Cooking time **10 minutes**

1 **garlic clove**, crushed
3 tablespoons **Greek yogurt**
200 g (7 oz) **feta cheese**,
   crumbled
20 g (¾ oz) **oregano leaves**,
   finely chopped
2 **aubergines**
**olive oil**, for brushing and
   drizzling
50 g (2 oz) **Sunblush
   tomatoes**
handful of **basil leaves**
**salt** and **pepper**

**Combine** the garlic, yogurt, feta and oregano in a bowl. Stir well, season to taste and set aside.

**Meanwhile**, slice the aubergines into slices 5 mm (¼ in) thick. Put a griddle pan over a high heat, brush the aubergine slices with a little oil and griddle, in batches, until they begin to char and soften.

**Spread** each aubergine slice with the yogurt mixture and top with a Sunblush tomato and a basil leaf. Roll the slices up, garnish with basil leaves, drizzle over a little olive oil and serve.

**For stuffed courgette rolls**, replace the aubergines with 2 large courgettes and grill as in the recipe above. Replace the oregano with chopped mint leaves and the Sunblush tomatoes with 50 g (2 oz) roasted red pepper (from a jar) sliced into strips, and garnish with mint leaves.

# roasted potato wedges with raita

Serves **4**
Preparation time **10 minutes**
Cooking time **20 minutes**

2 teaspoons **cumin seeds**
2 teaspoons **coriander seeds**
½ teaspoon **fenugreek seeds**
2 tablespoons **sunflower oil**
2 × 300 g (10 oz) packs
  **ready-prepared potato
  wedges**
¼ teaspoon **dried chilli flakes**
**salt** and **pepper**

**Raita**
200 ml (7 fl oz) **natural Greek
  yogurt**
15 g (½ oz) **mint**, chopped
¼ **cucumber**, finely diced

**Place** all the spices in a small, heavy-based frying pan and cook over a high heat for 1 minute, swirling the pan to toast the seeds evenly. Transfer to a mortar and grind with a pestle until finely ground. Mix the ground spices with the oil, then toss with the sweet potato wedges in a large bowl.

**Spread** the wedges out in a large roasting tin, season with salt and pepper and scatter with the chilli flakes. Place in a preheated oven, 200°C (400°F), Gas Mark 6, for 20 minutes until beginning to brown.

**Meanwhile**, mix together the ingredients for the raita and place in a small serving bowl.

**Remove** the roasted sweet potato wedges from the oven and serve with the raita for dipping.

**For sweet potato crisps**, heat 300 ml (½ pint) vegetable oil in a deep, heavy-based saucepan to 180–190°C (350–375°F), or until a cube of bread browns in 30 seconds. Meanwhile, thinly slice 2 peeled sweet potatoes with a mandolin or vegetable peeler. Deep-fry in small batches for 1–2 minutes until browned. Remove with a slotted spoon and drain on kitchen paper. Scatter over  salt and cumin seeds. Serve with the raita and some prepared fresh vegetables cut into chunks for dipping.

# camembert 'fondue' with honey & walnuts

Serves **4**
Preparation time **10 minutes**
Cooking time **5–10 minutes**

1 small **vegetarian
Camembert cheese**, in a
lidded box
6 **walnut halves**, roughly
chopped
2 tablespoons **thyme leaves**,
plus extra **thyme sprigs**, to
garnish
2 tablespoons **clear honey**
**crusty bread** and **vegetable
crudités**, to serve

**Remove** the cheese from its box and discard any paper or plastic wrapping. Slice off the top rind and replace the cheese in its box.

**Scatter** the walnuts and thyme over the surface of the cheese and drizzle with the honey.

**Replace** the lid and place the box in the centre of a preheated oven, 220°C (425°F), Gas Mark 7, for 5–10 minutes. Depending on the ripeness of the cheese, it should be nicely runny inside when cooked.

**Garnish** with thyme sprigs and serve warm with crusty bread and vegetable crudités.

**For camembert & walnut pasta**, cook 375 g (12 oz) penne according to the packet instructions. Drain and keep warm. Meanwhile finely slice 2 garlic cloves and 4 spring onions and stir-fry in a tablespoon olive oil in a large frying pan for 1–2 minutes. Add 2 chopped tomatoes and stir-fry for 5–6 minutes over a medium heat. Finely chop 2 tablespoons tarragon and add to the tomato mixture. Tip the drained pasta into the pan with 200 g (7 oz) chopped vegetarian Camembert cheese and 100 g (3½ oz) chopped toasted walnuts, and stir to mix well. Season and serve ladled into warmed bowls.

# spiced onion fritters with mint & coriander relish

Serves **4**
Preparation time **25 minutes**
Cooking time **10–15 minutes**

3–4 **onions**, sliced
1 teaspoon **red chilli powder**
1 teaspoon **ground turmeric**
2 teaspoons **cumin seeds**
1 tablespoon **coriander seeds**, crushed
250 g (8 oz) **chickpea flour**
**vegetable oil**, for deep-frying
**salt**

**Mint & coriander relish**
25 g (1 oz) **mint leaves**, finely chopped
20 g (¾ oz) **coriander leaves**, finely chopped
250 ml (8 fl oz) **natural yogurt**, whisked
1 tablespoon **lime juice**
1 tablespoon **mint jelly**

**First** make the relish by mixing all the ingredients together in a bowl, season well and chill until ready to serve.

**Separate** the sliced onions and place in a large bowl. Add the chilli powder, turmeric, cumin seeds, crushed coriander seeds and season with salt. Mix well. Add the chickpea flour a little at a time, stirring again to coat the onions. Gradually sprinkle some cold water over this mixture, adding just enough to make a sticky batter that coats the onions. Use your fingers to mix thoroughly.

**Fill** a deep, wide saucepan one-quarter full with vegetable oil and place over a high heat until it reaches 180°C (350°F) or a cube of bread sizzles and turns golden in 10–15 seconds.

**Drop** spoonfuls of the mixture into the oil. Fry in batches over medium–high heat for 1–2 minutes or until golden brown and crisp on the outside. Remove with a slotted spoon and drain on kitchen paper. Serve immediately with the relish.

# corn & bean tortilla stack

Serves **4**
Preparation time **20 minutes**
Cooking time **15 minutes**

2 **red peppers**, deseeded and
 chopped
2 tablespoons **olive oil**
1 × 400 g (13 oz) can
 **chopped tomatoes**
2 × 400 g (13 oz) cans
 **kidney beans**, drained
2 × 200 g (7 oz) cans
 **sweetcorn**, drained
½ teaspoon **chilli powder**
4 large **corn tortillas**
200g (7 oz) **vegetarian
 Cheddar cheese**, grated
1 tablespoon finely chopped
 **coriander leaves**, to garnish

**To serve**
**soured cream** (optional)
1 **avocado**, halved, stoned,
 peeled and sliced (optional)

**Place** the chopped peppers and olive oil in a large pan, cover and cook gently for 5 minutes. Add the tomatoes, beans, sweetcorn and chilli powder. Bring to the boil and simmer, uncovered, for 7–8 minutes until the mixture is quite thick.

**Place** 1 tortilla on a baking sheet. Top with one-third of the bean mixture and one-quarter of the cheese. Repeat this twice to make 3 layers and then place the final tortilla on top. Scatter over the remaining cheese and bake in a preheated oven, 190°C (375°F), Gas Mark 5, for 15 minutes.

**Garnish** with the chopped coriander leaves and serve with avocado and soured cream, if desired.

**For bean & corn wraps**, spread 4 corn tortillas with 2 tablespoons mayonnaise each. Mix together sweetcorn from 1 × 200 g (7 oz) can and 8 tablespoons kidney beans. Divide this mixture over the tortillas and scatter a tablespoon grated vegetarian Cheddar cheese over each of them. Roll up the tortillas to encase the filling and serve.

# chilli, tomato & rosemary cannellini beans on bruschetta

Serves **4**
Preparation time **15 minutes**
Cooking time **10 minutes**

3 tablespoons **extra virgin olive oil**, plus extra for drizzling
2 teaspoons chopped **rosemary leaves**
1 **red chilli**, chopped
2 × 400 g (13 oz) cans **cannellini beans**, drained
2 tablespoons chopped **Sunblush tomatoes**
8 slices **day-old bread from a sourdough loaf**
2 **garlic cloves**, halved
**salt** and **pepper**

**To garnish**
**basil leaves**
**lemon** wedges

**Heat** the oil in a frying pan over a low heat. Add the rosemary leaves and chilli and cook for a few seconds, until the mixture starts to sizzle. Add the beans and stir-fry for 2–3 minutes.

**Transfer** to a food processor and whizz until roughly combined. Season to taste with salt and pepper and fold in the chopped tomatoes.

**Heat** a griddle pan and warm the bread slices over a medium–high heat until lightly charred, or toast in a toaster. Rub the warm bread with the garlic halves and drizzle generously with olive oil. Scatter lightly with salt and top with the bean mixture.

**Season** with freshly ground black pepper and lightly drizzle again with oil. Garnish with basil leaves and lemon wedges.

**For tomato & chilli bean soup**, heat 2 × 400 g (13 oz) cans of cream of tomato soup and stir in 1 finely chopped red chilli and 1 × 400 g (13 oz) can cannellini beans, drained and rinsed. Bring to the boil and serve piping hot with toasted sourdough bread.

# creamy tarragon mushrooms on brioche toasts

8 slices **brioche**
150 g (5 oz) **butter**
2 **banana shallots**, finely chopped
3 **garlic cloves**, finely chopped
1 **red chilli**, deseeded and finely chopped (optional)
300 g (10 oz) **mixed wild mushrooms** (such as chanterelle, cep, girolle and oyster), trimmed and sliced
65 g (2½ oz) **crème fraîche**, plus extra to garnish (optional)
2 tablespoons finely chopped **tarragon**
1 tablespoon finely chopped **flat leaf parsley**
**salt** and **pepper**

**Lightly** toast the brioche slices and keep warm.

**Heat** the butter in a frying pan and sauté the shallots, garlic and chilli, if using, for 1–2 minutes. Now add the mushrooms and stir-fry over a moderate heat for 6–8 minutes. Season well, remove from the heat and stir in the crème fraîche and chopped herbs.

**Spoon** the mushrooms on to the sliced brioche and serve immediately, with an extra dollop of crème fraîche if desired.

**For mushroom & tarragon risotto**, bring 1.2 litres (2 pints) vegetable stock to the boil and keep hot. Meanwhile, heat 2 tablespoons olive oil in a large, heavy-based saucepan and add 1 chopped onion and 2 chopped garlic cloves. Fry over a gentle heat for 2–3 minutes, until softened. Add 250 g (8 oz) mixed wild mushrooms (as above) and fry for a further 2–3 minutes, until browned. Stir in 375 g (12 oz) arborio rice and stir to coat with the oil. Pour over 150 ml (¼ pint) dry white wine and simmer, stirring, until the liquid has been absorbed. Add a ladleful of the hot stock and simmer, stirring again, until the liquid has been absorbed. Continue adding the stock in this way, until all the liquid has been absorbed and the rice is plump and tender. Finish by stirring in 2 tablespoons each of chopped tarragon and parsley, and 40 g (1½ oz) butter. Season well and serve with freshly grated Parmesan-style vegetarian cheese.

# sweetcorn cakes with avocado salsa

Serves **4**
Preparation time **20 minutes**
Cooking time **10–15 minutes**

500 g (1 lb) **fresh sweetcorn kernels**
4 **spring onions**, finely sliced
2 **eggs**
20 g (¾ oz) **coriander leaves**, finely chopped, plus extra to garnish
125 g (4 oz) **plain flour**
1 teaspoon **baking powder**
**salt** and **pepper**
**vegetable oil**, for frying

**Avocado salsa**
2 ripe **avocados**, halved, stoned, peeled and finely diced
15 g (½ oz) each of chopped **mint** and **coriander leaves**
2 tablespoons **lime juice**
2 tablespoons finely chopped **red onion**
½ teaspoon **Tabasco sauce**

**Place** three-quarters of the sweetcorn kernels along with the spring onions, eggs, coriander, flour and baking powder in a food processor and whizz until combined. Season well and transfer to a large bowl. Add the remaining sweetcorn kernels and mix well.

**Heat** 1 tablespoon of vegetable oil in a large nonstick frying pan over a medium–high heat. When the oil is hot, drop heaped tablespoons of the mixture into the pan and cook in batches for 1 minute on each side.

**Drain** the sweetcorn cakes on kitchen paper and keep warm in a preheated oven, 120°C (250°F), Gas Mark ½, while making the rest of the cakes.

**To** make the avocado salsa, place all the ingredients in a bowl and stir very gently to combine.

**Serve** the warm sweetcorn cakes accompanied by the tangy avocado salsa and garnished with coriander leaves.

**For pea & mint fritters**, replace the sweetcorn in the recipe above with 500g (1 lb) thawed frozen peas and the coriander with 15 g (½ oz) chopped mint leaves and proceed as above. Stir 75 g (3 oz) natural yogurt into the salsa and serve with the pea and mint fritters.

# baked goats' cheese & pistachio with radicchio salad

Serves **4**
Preparation time **20 minutes**
Cooking time **12–15 minutes**

8 **vine leaves**, rinsed well in
   cold water
melted **butter**, for brushing
65 g (2½ oz) **pistachio nuts**
4 small **vegetarian Crottin de
   Chèvre**
4 teaspoons **white wine**

**Radicchio salad**
1 **garlic clove**, crushed
2 tablespoons **cider vinegar**
1 tablespoon **clear honey**
75 ml (3 fl oz) **extra virgin
   olive oil**
2 **pears**, cored and thinly
   sliced
2 small **radicchio**, leaves
   separated
**salt** and **pepper**

**Dry** the vine leaves, then on a clean work surface lay one flat and partly overlap another leaf side by side (by about one-third). Repeat with the other 6 vine leaves; you should end up with 4 pairs. Brush the leaves with a little melted butter and set aside. Whizz the pistachio nuts in a small food processor until coarsely ground.

**Brush** the cheeses with the remaining melted butter and then roll them in the chopped pistachios to coat. Place a cheese portion in the centre of each pair of leaves and sprinkle with the wine. Form a parcel by bringing the vine leaves up around each cheese and secure with string or cocktail sticks. Place the cheese parcels on a baking sheet and bake in a preheated oven, 160°C (325°F), Gas Mark 3, for 12–15 minutes.

**Meanwhile**, make the salad by whisking the garlic, vinegar, honey and seasoning together, then gradually whisk in the oil. Toss with the pear and radicchio leaves.

**Serve** the crottins, still in their vine leaf wrappings to be unwrapped at the table, accompanied by the salad.

**For goats' cheese, pear & pistachio melts**, rub 4 large slices sourdough bread with 2 halved garlic cloves and drizzle each with 1 tablespoon olive oil. Thinly slice 1 pear and arrange over the bread. Scatter over 100 g (3½ oz) chopped pistachio nuts and cover with thin slices from 2 small vegetarian Crottin de Chèvre. Melt under a hot grill for 2 minutes and serve with a radicchio salad.

# greek salad with toasted pitta

Serves **4**
Preparation time **15 minutes**
Cooking time **5 minutes**

100 g (3½ oz) **vegetarian feta cheese**, crumbled into smallish chunks
8–10 **mint leaves**, shredded
100 g (3½ oz) **kalamata olives**, pitted
2 **tomatoes**, chopped
juice of a large **lemon**
1 small **red onion**, thinly sliced
1 teaspoon **dried oregano**
4 **pitta breads**
**lemon** wedges, to serve

**In** a bowl, toss together the feta, mint, olives, tomatoes, lemon juice, onion and oregano.

**Toast** the pittas under a preheated hot grill until lightly golden, then split open and toast the open sides.

**Tear** the hot pittas into bite-sized pieces, then toss with the other ingredients in the bowl. Serve with lemon wedges.

**For grilled feta, spinach & pine nut salad**, place 200 g (7 oz) block vegetarian feta cheese on a baking sheet and scatter over 1 teaspoon dried oregano. Place under a preheated hot grill for 5–6 minutes or until lightly browned. Meanwhile put 300 g (10 oz) of baby spinach into a wide bowl with 1 sliced red onion, 2 chopped tomatoes and 25 g (1 oz) toasted pine nuts. Scatter over 2 tablespoons sherry vinegar, then drizzle with 75 ml (3 fl oz) olive oil. Season well and toss. Cut the grilled feta into small cubes, scatter over the salad and serve.

# spinach & potato tortilla

Serves **4**
Preparation time **10 minutes**
Cooking time **14–18 minutes**

3 tablespoons **olive oil**
2 **onions**, finely chopped
250 g (8 oz) cooked **potatoes**,
  peeled and cut into 1 cm
  (½ in) cubes
2 **garlic cloves**, finely chopped
200 g (7 oz) cooked **spinach**,
  drained thoroughly and
  roughly chopped
50 g (2 oz) **roasted red
  pepper from a jar**, finely
  chopped
5 **eggs**, lightly beaten
25 g (1 oz) **vegetarian
  Manchego cheese**, grated
**salt** and **pepper**

**Heat** the oil in a large nonstick frying pan and add the onions and potatoes. Cook gently over a medium heat for 3–4 minutes or until the vegetables have softened but not coloured, turning and stirring often.

**Add** the garlic, spinach and roasted pepper and stir to mix well.

**Beat** the eggs lightly and season well. Pour into the frying pan, shaking the pan so that the eggs are evenly spread. Cook gently for 8–10 minutes or until the tortilla is set at the bottom.

**Scatter** over the grated Manchego. Place the frying pan under a preheated medium-hot grill and cook for 3–4 minutes or until the top is set and golden.

**Remove** from the heat, cut into bite-sized squares or triangles and serve warm or at room temperature.

**For spinach & potato sauté**, heat 1 tablespoon vegetable oil in a large frying pan. Add 2 chopped garlic cloves, 1 finely chopped onion and 1 tablespoon curry powder. Stir in 100 ml (3½ fl oz) passata, 300 g (10 oz) baby spinach and 200 g (7 oz) cooked, cubed potatoes. Sauté over a high heat for 2–3 minutes or until piping hot. Season and serve with crusty bread or rice.

# hot-crumbed mozzarella balls with fresh pesto aïoli

Serves **4**
Preparation time **10 minutes**
Cooking time **5 minutes**

100 g (3½ oz) **fresh white breadcrumbs**
zest of 1 **lemon**, finely grated
generous pinch of **chilli flakes**
2 tablespoons **thyme leaves**
50 g (2 oz) **plain flour**
2 large **eggs**, beaten
300 g (10 oz) **vegetarian bocconcini** (baby mozzarella balls), drained
**vegetable oil**, for deep-frying
**salt** and **pepper**

**Fresh pesto aïoli**
100 g (3½ oz) **fresh ready-made vegetarian pesto**
200 g (7 oz) **fresh mayonnaise**
2 **garlic cloves**, crushed

**Make** the pesto aïoli by mixing together all the ingredients. Set aside.

**In** a medium bowl, mix together the breadcrumbs, lemon zest, a few chilli flakes, a scattering of the thyme and some seasoning. Place the flour in a second bowl and the eggs in a third.

**Pat** the mozzarella balls dry with kitchen paper. Roll the balls first in flour, then dip in the eggs and roll in the breadcrumb mixture. Repeat in the eggs and breadcrumbs to create a double layer.

**Half** fill a saucepan or deep-fat fryer with vegetable oil. Just before serving, heat over a high heat until it reaches 180°C (350°F) or a cube of bread sizzles and turns golden in 10–15 seconds. Using a slotted spoon, lower the crumbed mozzarella balls into the hot oil and fry for 3–4 minutes until golden brown. Remove and drain on kitchen paper.

**Serve** immediately with the fresh pesto aïoli.

**For tomato, bocconcini & basil tricolore salad**, slice 4 tomatoes and place in a wide salad bowl with a small handful of basil leaves and 300 g (10 oz) vegetarian bocconcini. Drizzle over 50 ml (2 fl oz) extra virgin olive oil and squeeze over the juice of 1 lemon. Season well and serve with ciabatta bread.

# spiced paneer bruschettas

Serves **4**
Preparation time **15 minutes**
Cooking time **5 minutes**

200 g (7 oz) fresh **vegetarian
  paneer** (Indian cheese)
  or **feta cheese**, roughly
  chopped
3 tablespoons finely chopped
  **red onion**
1 **green chilli**, deseeded and
  finely sliced
large handful of **coriander**,
  finely chopped
150 g (5 oz) baby **plum
  tomatoes**, quartered
2 tablespoons **extra virgin
  olive oil**, plus extra for
  drizzling (optional)
juice and finely grated zest of
  1 **lime**
12 slices **ciabatta bread**
**salt** and **pepper**

**Place** the cheese in a mixing bowl. Add the onion, chilli,
coriander, tomatoes, olive oil, lime juice and zest and
then season. Stir well and allow to sit while you toast or
griddle the ciabatta slices.

**Spoon** the cheese mixture over the toasted ciabatta
slices and serve immediately, drizzled with extra olive oil
if desired.

**For spiced paneer skewers**, cut 500 g (1 lb)
vegetarian paneer into 5 cm (2 in) cubes. Scatter
over 1 tablespoon each of chilli powder and salt.
Toss everything together and ensure the paneer is
evenly coated. Combine 2 tablespoons chickpea flour
with 2 teaspoons cumin seeds and 75 ml (3 fl oz)
double cream. Coat the cubes in the spiced cream
and marinate for 10 minutes. Thread on to 4 metal
skewers and cook under a preheated hot grill for
1–2 minutes on each side. Serve garnished with
chopped coriander leaves and a salad.

# spring onion rostis with avocado, red onion & tomato salsa

Serves **4**
Preparation time **25 minutes**
Cooking time **15 minutes**

875 g (1¾ lb) boiled
   **potatoes**, such as **King
   Edward** or **Maris Piper**
6 **spring onions**, finely
   chopped
2 **garlic cloves**, very finely
   chopped
1 large **egg**, lightly beaten
50 ml (2 fl oz) **sunflower oil**
**lime** wedges, to serve

**Avocado, red onion & tomato
   salsa**
2 **plum tomatoes**, deseeded
   and roughly chopped
1 **red chilli**, deseeded and
   finely chopped
1 small **red onion**, halved and
   very thinly sliced
15 g (½ oz) **coriander**, finely
   chopped
2 **avocados**, halved, stoned,
   peeled and roughly diced
juice of 2 **limes**
1 tablespoon **avocado oil**

**First** make the salsa by mixing all the ingredients together in a bowl. Season well and set aside until ready to serve.

**Peel** and coarsely grate the potatoes. Add the spring onions, garlic and egg and use your fingers to combine evenly.

**Heat** a large, nonstick frying pan over a high heat and add half of the oil.

**Divide** the potato mixture into 8 portions. Lower 4 of the portions into the oil and pat down to form rostis 8–10 cm (3¼–4 in) in diameter. Cook for 3–4 minutes on each side and then carefully transfer to a plate. Repeat with the remaining oil and potato mixture to make 8 rostis. **Serve** the rostis accompanied the salsa and lime wedges.

**For fresh salsa & pasta salad**, cook 300 g (10 oz) short-shaped pasta according to the packet instructions. Meanwhile finely chop 4 plum tomatoes, 1 red chilli, 1 red onion and 20 g (¾ oz) coriander leaves and place in a wide bowl. Peel, stone and roughly dice 2 avocados and add to the bowl with the drained pasta. Drizzle over 50 ml (2 fl oz) extra virgin olive oil and the juice of 2 limes. Season, toss to mix well and serve.

# corn & courgette cakes

Serves **4**
Preparation time **15 minutes**
Cooking time **10–15 minutes**

150 g (5 oz) fresh **sweetcorn kernels**
1 **courgette**, coarsely grated
1 teaspoon **cumin seeds**
4 **spring onions**, thinly sliced
3 tablespoons **self raising flour**
2 **eggs**, beaten
2 tablespoons chopped **coriander**
1 **red chilli**, deseeded and roughly chopped
**vegetable oil**, for shallow-frying
**salt** and **pepper**

**To serve**
**ready-made guacamole**
**lime** wedges

**Place** the corn in a large bowl with the courgette, cumin seeds, spring onions, flour, eggs, coriander, chilli and some seasoning and mix well.

**Heat** a tablespoon of vegetable oil in a large nonstick frying pan and cook spoonfuls of the mixture in batches for 2–3 minutes on each side until cooked through. You should end up with 12 cakes, 3 for each person.

**Serve** with guacamole and lime wedges.

**For creamy courgette & corn pasta bake**, cook 250 g (8 oz) dried rigatoni according to the packet instructions, then drain and set aside in a large mixing bowl. Meanwhile, heat 2 tablespoons olive oil in a large frying pan and sauté 1 chopped onion and 2 chopped garlic cloves for 1–2 minutes. Add 1 finely diced courgette and 400 g (13 oz) fresh sweetcorn kernels and stir-fry for another minute or so. Mix 200 ml (7 fl oz) crème fraîche with 2 beaten eggs and a tablespoon Dijon mustard. Season well and add to the pasta with the vegetable mixture and 15 g (½ oz) chopped coriander. Mix well, transfer to a shallow ovenproof dish and bake in a preheated oven, 200°C (400°F), Gas Mark 6, for 12–15 minutes. Remove from the oven and serve.

# brie & thyme melts

Serves **4**
Preparation time **10 minutes**
Cooking time **3–4 minutes**

1 **ciabatta-style loaf**, cut in
  half horizontally
125 g (4 oz) **onion** or
  **caramelized onion chutney**
200 g (7 oz) **vegetarian Brie**
  or **Camembert cheese**,
  sliced
1 teaspoon **dried thyme**
4 teaspoons **chilli**, **garlic** or
  **basil oil**
**tomato salad**, to serve
  (optional)

**Cut** the two pieces of bread in half to give 4 portions. Arrange, cut side up, on a baking sheet and spread each piece with the onion chutney.

**Lay** the Brie slices on top and scatter over the thyme. Drizzle with the flavoured oil and cook under a preheated grill for 3–4 minutes, until the cheese begins to melt. Serve immediately with a tomato salad, if desired.

**For brie, thyme & onion tart**, place 375 g (12 oz) ready-rolled shortcrust pastry on a large greased baking sheet and fold in the edges by about 1 cm (½ in) to create a crust. Spread with 125 g (4 oz) onion chutney, then top with 200 g (7 oz) sliced vegetarian Brie or Camembert cheese. Scatter 1 teaspoon dried thyme over the cheese and drizzle with 4 teaspoons chilli, garlic or basil oil. Cook in a preheated oven, 200°C (400°F), Gas Mark 6, for about 20 minutes until the pastry is crisp and golden and the cheese has melted. Serve with a tomato salad.

# vegetable spring rolls

Serves **4**
Preparation time **10 minutes**
Cooking time **15–18 minutes**

1 tablespoon **groundnut oil**
2 **garlic cloves**, finely chopped
small piece of **fresh root
ginger**, grated
1 **red chilli**, deseeded and
finely chopped
300 g (10 oz) bag **mixed
stir-fry vegetables**
1 tablespoon **soy sauce**
1 tablespoon **rice wine
vinegar**
4 sheets **filo pastry**, each cut
into 4 rectangles (about
15 × 12 cm/6 × 5 in)
50 g (2 oz) **salted butter**,
melted
**sweet chilli sauce**, to serve

**Heat** a wok over a high heat and add the oil, garlic,
ginger and chilli, then stir-fry for 30 seconds. Add the
mixed vegetables, soy sauce and vinegar and cook for
1 minute. Spoon the vegetables into a sieve over a bowl
and allow to cool slightly.

**Place** a spoonful of the vegetable mixture in the centre
of the narrow edge of a filo rectangle. Roll the filo
around the mixture until halfway along the filo sheet,
then fold each side of unfilled pastry into the centre.
Continue rolling into a cylinder and brush with butter
to seal. Repeat with the remaining pastry sheets.

**Place** the spring rolls on a baking tray and brush
with melted butter. Bake in a preheated oven, 200°C
(400°F), Gas Mark 6, for 12–15 minutes until golden
and crisp. Serve hot with sweet chilli sauce.

**For vegetable fried rice**, heat 2 tablespoons
vegetable oil in a large frying pan or wok over a
high heat. Add 2 chopped garlic cloves, 1 teaspoon
coarsely grated ginger, 500 g (1 lb) cooked white rice
and a 300 g (10 oz) pack mixed stir-fry vegetables.
Stir-fry over a high heat for 5–6 minutes or until piping
hot. Stir in 75 ml (3 fl oz) light soy sauce, 1 tablespoon
sesame oil and 1 teaspoon chilli oil. Remove from the
heat, stir in the juice of 1 lime and serve immediately.

# soups & salads

# bulgur salad with roasted peppers on little gem leaves

Serves **4**
Preparation time **10 minutes**
Cooking time **10–15 minutes**

200 g (7 oz) **fine bulgur
wheat**
1 tablespoon **tomato purée**
juice of 1 ½ **lemons**
75 ml (3 fl oz) **extra virgin
olive oil**
1 **red chilli**, finely chopped
200 g (7 oz) **roasted red
peppers** (from a jar), drained
and diced
8 **spring onions**, finely sliced
300 g (10 oz) **tomatoes**, diced
50 g (2 oz) **flat leaf parsley**,
roughly chopped
25 g (1 oz) **mint leaves**,
roughly chopped
4 **Little Gem lettuces**, leaves
separated
**salt**

**Tip** the bulgur wheat into a bowl, pour over 125 ml (4 fl oz) boiling water, stir, then cover and leave for 10–15 minutes until the grains are tender.

**Add** the tomato purée, lemon juice, olive oil, the red chilli and some salt to the bulgur wheat mixture and mix thoroughly.

**Add** the roasted red peppers, spring onions and tomatoes, together with the parsley and mint, and mix well.

**Arrange** the lettuce leaves around the edges of a platter with the bulgur salad in the centre. Use the leaves to scoop up the bulgur mixture and eat.

### For layered roasted red pepper, bulgur and tomato
**pot**, prepare the bulgur wheat mixture as above and tip into a medium-sized shallow ovenproof dish with 200 g (7 oz) diced roasted red pepper (from a jar), drained. Slice 4 plum tomatoes and place over the bulgur wheat to cover. Scatter over 1 finely chopped red chilli and drizzle over 50 ml (2 fl oz) olive oil. Cook under a preheated medium grill for 5 minutes. Crumble 150 g (5 oz) feta cheese on top and scatter over 8 chopped pitted black olives. Return the dish to the grill for 4–5 minutes or until the feta is browned. Serve immediately.

# spiced potato, coriander & celeriac soup

Serves **4**
Preparation time **15 minutes**
Cooking time **16–21 minutes**

1 **onion**, chopped
2 tablespoons **olive oil**
1 **garlic clove**, chopped
½ teaspoon each of **ground cumin** and **coriander**
pinch of **chilli flakes**
2 small **celeriac**, peeled and finely diced
2 medium **potatoes**, peeled and finely diced
1 litre (1¾ pint) hot **vegetable stock**
25 g (1 oz) **coriander**, chopped

**To serve**
65 g (2½ oz) **crème fraîche**
toasted **cumin seeds**

**Place** the onion and olive oil in a pan with the garlic, ground cumin and coriander and a pinch of chilli flakes. Fry over a medium heat for 1 minute.

**Add** the celeriac and potatoes, cover with the hot vegetable stock and bring to the boil. Simmer for 15–20 minutes or until the vegetables are tender.

**Stir** in the chopped coriander and blend with a hand-held blender until fairly smooth.

**Serve** in warmed bowls with a dollop of crème fraîche and toasted cumin seeds.

**For celeriac, carrot & cabbage slaw**, mix 1 coarsely grated celeriac, 2 coarsely grated carrots, ½ finely shredded red cabbage and a large handful of chopped coriander leaves together in a large bowl. Mix 100 ml (3½ fl oz) crème fraiche together with 150 g (5 oz) mayonnaise, 1 teaspoon each of ground cumin, ground coriander and dried chilli flakes, and the juice of 2 limes. Season, pour over the celeriac mixture, toss to mix well and serve.

# chunky mushroom soup

Serves **4**
Preparation time **10 minutes**
Cooking time **15–20 minutes**

25 g (1 oz) **butter**
1 large **onion**, chopped
1 **leek**, finely sliced
2 **garlic cloves**, crushed
300 g (10 oz) **chestnut
mushrooms**, roughly
chopped
2 tablespoons **plain flour**
500 ml (17 fl oz) **vegetable
stock**
400 ml (14 fl oz) **milk**
1 tablespoon finely chopped
**tarragon**
**salt** and **pepper**
**crusty bread**, to serve

**Melt** the butter in a pan over a low heat and gently fry
the onion, leek and garlic until they start to soften.

**Increase** the heat and add the mushrooms to the pan,
stirring until well combined. Continue to fry, stirring, for
2–3 minutes.

**Stir** in the flour and continue to cook for 1 minute.

**Remove** the pan from the heat and add the stock a
little at a time, stirring well between each addition.

**Once** all the stock is added, return the pan to the heat,
bring to the boil, reduce the heat and simmer for a few
minutes.

**Pour** in the milk and bring to a simmer. Stir in the
chopped tarragon and season to taste.

**Ladle** the soup into bowls and serve with crusty bread.

**For mushroom stir-fry**, heat 2 tablespoons butter
in a large wok and add 300 g (10 oz) sliced chestnut
mushrooms, 2 chopped garlic cloves, 1 sliced onion and
1 sliced leek. Stir-fry over a high heat for 6–8 minutes,
remove from the heat, stir in 50 ml (2 fl oz) light soy sauce
and serve over noodles or rice.

# lettuce, pea & tarragon soup

Serves **4**
Preparation time **10 minutes**
Cooking time **10 minutes**

2 tablespoons **butter**
8 **spring onions**, trimmed and
  sliced
750 g (1½ lb) **frozen peas**
1 tablespoon chopped
  **tarragon leaves**
1 **romaine lettuce**, finely
  shredded
1 litre (1¾ pints) hot
  **vegetable stock**
**salt** and **pepper**

**To serve**
2 tablespoons **double cream**
**tarragon sprigs**, to garnish
  (optional)

**Melt** the butter in a large saucepan over a medium heat.
Add the spring onions and cook, stirring continuously,
for 2 minutes.

**Stir** in the peas, half of the tarragon and the lettuce.
Cook for 1 minute.

**Add** the stock, bring to the boil, cover and simmer for
5 minutes or until tender.

**Pour** the soup into a blender, add the remaining
tarragon and whizz until smooth. Season to taste.

**Divide** the soup among 4 bowls, swirl the cream into
each bowl and season with black pepper. Garnish with
tarragon sprigs, if liked.

**For quinoa and lettuce tabouleh**, put 200 g (7 oz)
quinoa into a saucepan and dry-fry for 2–3 minutes.
Add 600 ml (1 pint) hot vegetable stock, bring to the
boil and stir to mix well. Reduce the heat and cook for
15–20 minutes or until all the liquid has been absorbed.
Meanwhile, roughly chop the leaves of 1 romaine lettuce
and add to a wide salad bowl with 6 finely chopped spring
onions, 15 g (½ oz) each of finely chopped tarragon
and parsley, and 400 g (13 oz) blanched peas. Transfer
the quinoa to the bowl and drizzle over 75 ml (3 fl oz)
olive oil and the juice of 1 orange. Season, toss to mix
well and serve.

# hearty minestrone

Serves **4**
Preparation time **20 minutes**
Cooking time **12–15 minutes**

3 **carrots**, roughly chopped
1 **red onion**, roughly chopped
6 **celery stalks**, roughly
chopped
2 tablespoons **olive oil**
2 **garlic cloves**, crushed
200 g (7 oz) **potatoes**, peeled
and cut into 1 cm (½ in) dice
65 g (2½ oz) **tomato purée**
1.5 litres (2½ pints) **vegetable
stock**
1 × 400 g (13 oz) can
**chopped tomatoes**
150 g (5 oz) **dried short-
shaped soup pasta**
1 × 400 g (13 oz) can
**cannellini beans**, drained
100 g (3½ oz) **baby spinach**
**salt** and **pepper**

**Whizz** the carrots, onion and celery in a food processor until finely chopped.

**Heat** the oil in a large saucepan, add the chopped vegetables, garlic, potatoes, tomato purée, stock, chopped tomatoes and pasta. Bring to the boil, reduce the heat and simmer, covered, for 12–15 minutes.

**Tip** in the cannellini beans and the spinach for the final 2 minutes of cooking time.

**Season** to taste and serve with crusty bread.

**For chunky pasta sauce**, heat 2 tablespoons olive oil in a large frying pan and add 2 chopped garlic cloves, 1 chopped red onion, 2 chopped celery stalks, 1 chopped carrot and 1 × 400 g (13 oz) can chopped tomatoes. Bring to the boil and simmer for 12–15 minutes. Meanwhile, cook 375 g (12 oz) dried short-shaped pasta according to the packet instructions. Stir 100 g (3½ oz) baby spinach into the sauce with 200 g (7 oz) drained cannellini beans. Season well and serve over the cooked pasta with grated Parmesan-style vegetarian cheese.

# spiced corn chowder

Serves **4**
Preparation time **15 minutes**
Cooking time **20–25 minutes**

1 tablespoon **olive oil**
1 large **onion**, finely chopped
2 **garlic cloves**, finely chopped
1 teaspoon **cayenne pepper**
200 g (7 oz) **red split lentils**,
  rinsed
1 litre (1¾ pints) hot
  **vegetable stock**
1 × 400 ml (14 fl oz) can
  **coconut milk**
1 **Scotch bonnet chilli**, left
  whole
1 tablespoon **thyme leaves**
200 g (7 oz) **potatoes**, peeled
  and cut into 1 cm (½ in) dice
200 g (7 oz) **carrots**, peeled
  and cut into 1 cm (½ in) dice
400 g (13 oz) **sweetcorn
  kernels** (either fresh, frozen
  or canned)
2 **red peppers**, cut into 1 cm
  (½ in) dice
**salt** and **pepper**
chopped **coriander**, to garnish

**Heat** the oil in a saucepan and stir-fry the onion and garlic for 2–3 minutes.

**Increase** the heat, add the cayenne pepper, red lentils, stock, coconut milk, chilli, thyme, potatoes and carrots. Bring to the boil and simmer for 15–20 minutes.

**Season** and add the corn and red pepper for the last 3 minutes of cooking.

**Remove** the Scotch bonnet chilli, ladle the chowder into warmed bowls and serve garnished with chopped coriander and seasoned with freshly ground black pepper.

**For spicy corn hash**, heat 1 tablespoon olive oil in a large frying pan. Add 1 chopped onion, 2 chopped garlic cloves, ¼ chopped Scotch bonnet chilli (you might want to wear washing-up gloves to do this as they're fiercely hot) and 1 teaspoon cayenne pepper. Stir-fry for 1–2 minutes and then add 200 g (7 oz) each coarsely grated potatoes and carrots, 500 g (1 lb) sweetcorn kernels and 1 finely diced red pepper. Add 200 ml (7 fl oz) coconut milk, stir and cook over a high heat for 10 minutes or until the liquid has evaporated and the vegetables are tender. Garnish with chopped coriander before serving with crusty bread and a fried egg, if desired.

# broth with rice, egg & greens

Serves **4**
Preparation time **15 minutes**
Cooking time **15–20 minutes**

4 **spring onions**
100 g (3½ oz) **pak choi**,
   roughly chopped
2 tablespoons **vegetable oil**
2.5 cm (1 in) piece of **fresh
   root ginger**, finely grated
2 **garlic cloves**, finely chopped
200 g (7 oz) **Thai fragrant
   jasmine rice**
100 ml (3½ fl oz) **rice wine**
2 tablespoons **soy sauce**
1 teaspoon **rice wine vinegar**
1 litre (1¾ pints) hot
   **vegetable stock**
4 **eggs**
1 tablespoon **chilli oil**, for
   drizzling

**Finely** slice the spring onions, keeping the white and green parts separate. Combine the green bits with the pak choi in a bowl and set aside.

**Heat** the oil gently in a saucepan. When hot, add the onion whites, ginger and garlic and stir-fry for 2–3 minutes.

**Add** the rice, stir, then add the wine and bubble for a minute or so.

**Add** the soy sauce, vinegar and stock and simmer, stirring occasionally, for 10–12 minutes. Then stir in the reserved spring onions and pak choi and cook for 2–3 minutes.

**Meanwhile,** poach the eggs in two batches.

**Ladle** the soup into 4 soup bowls and top each one with a poached egg and drizzle over the chilli oil.

**For egg noodle and vegetable stir-fry**, heat 2 tablespoons vegetable oil in a large wok and add 8 sliced spring onions, 1 sliced red pepper, 2 chopped garlic cloves and 1 teaspoon finely chopped fresh root ginger. Stir-fry over a medium heat for 3–4 minutes. Add 400 g (13 oz) roughly chopped pak choi and stir-fry for a further 2–3 minutes. In a bowl, mix together 1 tablespoon cornflour with 75 ml (3 fl oz) light soy sauce, 100 ml (3½ fl oz) vegetable stock, 1 teaspoon chilli oil and 50 ml (2 fl oz) rice wine vinegar. Pour into the wok, turn the heat to high and cook for 2–3 minutes. Add 400 g (13 oz) cooked fresh egg noodles, toss to mix well and heat until piping hot. Serve immediately.

# spinach & red lentil soup

Serves **4**
Preparation time **10 minutes**
Cooking time **15 minutes**

250 g (8 oz) dried **red lentils**
3 tablespoons **sunflower oil**
1 large **onion**, finely chopped
2 **garlic cloves**, crushed
2.5 cm (1 in) piece of **fresh
root ginger**, grated
1 **red chilli**, deseeded and
chopped, plus extra to
garnish (optional)
1 tablespoon **medium curry
powder**
300 ml (½ pint) hot **vegetable
stock**
200 g (7 oz) canned
**tomatoes**
100 g (3½ oz) **baby spinach**
25 g (1 oz) **coriander leaves**,
chopped, plus extra to
garnish
100 ml (3½ fl oz) **coconut
cream**
**salt** and **pepper**
65 g (2½ oz) **natural yogurt**,
to serve

**Put** the lentils into a medium saucepan and cover
with 900 ml (1 ½ pints) cold water. Bring to the boil,
skimming off the scum as it rises to the surface, and
leave to simmer for 10 minutes until the lentils are
tender and just falling apart. Remove from the heat,
cover and set aside.

**Meanwhile,** heat the oil in a large saucepan, add the
onion and fry gently for 5 minutes. Add the garlic, ginger
and chilli and fry for a further 2 minutes. Stir in the curry
powder and ½ teaspoon black pepper and cook for a
further 2 minutes.

**Add** the stock, the lentils and their cooking liquid, the
tomatoes, spinach and coriander and season with salt
to taste. Cover and simmer for 5 minutes then add the
coconut cream.

**Whizz** the mixture with a hand-held blender, until the
soup is almost smooth.

**Ladle** the soup into 4 warmed bowls, swirl each with
a spoonful of yogurt and garnish with coriander leaves,
freshly ground black pepper and finely chopped red
chilli, if desired.

# mixed beans & baby spinach salad with avocado dressing

Serves **4**
Preparation time **10 minutes**
Cooking time **2–3 minutes**

150 g (5 oz) **baby spinach**
1 large **carrot**, coarsely grated
150 g (5 oz) medium **vine tomatoes**, quartered
1 small **red pepper**, deseeded and thinly sliced
1 × 400 g (13 oz) can **mixed beans**, drained
100 g (3½ oz) canned **chickpeas**, drained
2 tablespoons **pumpkin seeds**, lightly toasted

**Avocado dressing**
1 ripe **avocado**
1 teaspoon **Dijon mustard**
juice of 1 **lemon**
1 teaspoon **clear honey**
dash of **Tabasco sauce**
50 ml (2 fl oz) **extra virgin olive oil**
**salt** and **pepper**

**Mix** the baby spinach leaves and carrot together and place on a wide salad platter or into a large bowl.

**Add** the tomatoes and pepper slices and scatter over the mixed beans, chickpeas and toasted pumpkin seeds.

**Halve** the avocado and remove the stone. Scoop the flesh into a food processor and add the mustard, lemon juice, honey and Tabasco sauce. Blend until smooth then, with the motor still running, gradually pour in the oil and 2–3 tablespoons warm water. Season to taste.

**Drizzle** the dressing over the salad and serve immediately.

**For rustic mixed bean and spinach soup**, heat 2 × 400 g (13 oz) cans of cream of tomato soup in a large saucepan, then add 1 × 400 g (13 oz) can of mixed beans (drained) and 200 g (7 oz) chopped baby spinach and bring to the boil. Simmer gently for 5–6 minutes, season and serve immediately.

# tricolore avocado & couscous salad

Serves **4**
Preparation time **5 minutes**
Cooking time **10 minutes**

200 g (7 oz) **couscous**
300 ml (½ pint) hot **vegetable stock** or boiling **water**
2 **avocados**
250 g (8 oz) **cherry tomatoes**, halved
150 g (5 oz) **vegetarian mozzarella cheese**, drained and chopped
handful of **rocket leaves**

**Pesto dressing**
2 tablespoons **vegetarian green pesto**
1 tablespoon **lemon juice**
50 ml (2 fl oz) **extra virgin olive oil**
**salt** and **pepper**

**Mix** the couscous and stock (or boiling water) together in a bowl, then cover with a plate and leave for 10 minutes.

**To** make the dressing, mix the pesto with the lemon juice and season, then gradually mix in the oil. Pour over the couscous and mix with a fork.

**Halve**, stone, peel and chop the avocados. Add the chopped avocados together with the tomatoes and mozzarella to the couscous, mix well, then lightly stir in the rocket.

**For Italian-style ciabatta with cherry tomatoes, avocado and mozzarella**, mix together 250 g (8 oz) chopped tomatoes, 2 chopped avocados, 200 g (7 oz) chopped vegetarian mozzarella and season well. Halve and lighty toast 4 ciabatta rolls and spread with 8 tablespoons ready-made vegetarian pesto. Divide the avocado mixture among the rolls, garnish with a few rocket leaves and serve.

# veggie caesar-style salad

Serves **4**
Preparation time **20 minutes**
Cooking time **10–12 minutes**

2 **red apples**, cored and diced
4 **celery stalks**, thinly sliced
1 head of **cos lettuce**, leaves
   washed and roughly torn
4 **spring onions**, thinly sliced
bunch of **chives**, chopped
4 hard-boiled **eggs**, shelled
   and halved, to garnish

**Croutons**
2 slices of **crusty bread**, cubed
2 teaspoons **garlic salt**
2 teaspoons **dried mixed herbs**
3 tablespoons **olive oil**

**Caesar-style dressing**
2 **garlic cloves**, crushed
2 tablespoons **capers**, drained
2 tablespoons **lemon juice**
2 teaspoons **Dijon mustard**
1 teaspoon **clear honey**
65 g (2½ oz) **Parmesan-style
   vegetarian cheese**, grated
100 ml (3½ fl oz) **natural
   yogurt**
**salt** and **pepper**

**First** make the croutons. Place the cubes of bread in a bowl and scatter over the garlic salt and dried herbs. Drizzle with the olive oil and toss to coat evenly.

**Place** the croutons on a baking sheet in a single layer and bake in a preheated oven, 200°C (400°F), Gas Mark 6, for 10–12 minutes or until lightly browned and crisp. Remove from the oven and set aside.

**Meanwhile**, make the dressing. Place the garlic, capers, lemon juice, mustard, honey, Parmesan and yogurt in a blender and whizz until smooth. Season with black pepper. Chill until ready to use (you can make the dressing up to a day in advance, if desired).

**Place** the apples, celery, lettuce, spring onions and chives in a wide salad bowl.

**Drizzle** most of the dressing over the salad ingredients and toss to mix well.

**Top** with the halved eggs and the garlic and herb croutons, then drizzle with the remaining dressing and season with black pepper.

**For crisp lettuce salad with croutons**, place the leaves from 2 romaine or cos lettuces in a bowl with 6 sliced spring onions, 2 sliced celery stalks and 1 sliced cucumber. Drizzle over 125 ml (4 fl oz) ready-made vegetarian Caesar salad dressing, scatter over 100 g (3½ oz) ready-made croutons, season, toss to mix well and serve.

# broccoli & lemon pasta salad

Serves **4**
Preparation time **10 minutes**
Cooking time **10 minutes**

375 g (12 oz) **dried penne** or
  **rigatoni**
150 g (5 oz) **broccoli florets**
100 g (3½ oz) **frozen**
  **edamame beans**
100 g (3½ oz) **frozen peas**
100 g (3½ oz) **sugarsnap**
  **peas**, trimmed
150 g (5 oz) **soft cheese with**
  **garlic and herbs**
finely grated zest and juice of
  **1 lemon**
50 ml (2 fl oz) **olive oil**
1 **red chilli**, deseeded and
  finely chopped
100 g (3½ oz) **Parmesan-**
  **style vegetarian cheese**,
  grated
2 tablespoons chopped
  **tarragon leaves**
**salt** and **pepper**

**Cook** the pasta in a large saucepan following the packet instructions, adding the broccoli florets, edamame beans, peas and sugarsnaps for the final 3 minutes of its cooking time.

**Drain** the pasta and vegetables, saving a ladleful of the cooking water, then tip back into the pan.

**Stir** in the soft cheese, lemon zest and juice, olive oil, chilli, Parmesan, tarragon, some seasoning and a splash of cooking water.

**Serve** the salad warm or at room temperature.

**For quick broccoli and vegetable stir-fry**, heat 2 tablespoons olive oil in a large wok. Add 300 g (10 oz) blanched broccoli florets, 100 g (3½ oz) edamame beans, 100 g (3½ oz) peas, 100 g (3½ oz) sugarsnap peas, 2 crushed garlic cloves, 1 chopped red chilli and 1 teaspoon grated fresh root ginger. Stir-fry over a high heat for 4–5 minutes, then stir in a 100 g (3½ oz) sachet of ready-made vegetarian stir-fry sauce of your choice. Stir-fry for 2–3 minutes and serve immediately over cooked noodles.

# roasted vegetable & bulgur salad

Serves **4**
Preparation time **15 minutes**
Cooking time **20 minutes**

2 tablespoons **harissa paste**
2 tablespoons **olive oil**
500 g (1 lb) **butternut squash**
  and **sweet potato**, diced
2 **red peppers**, deseeded and
  cut into bite-sized pieces
125 g (4 oz) **bulgur wheat**
600 ml (1 pint) hot **vegetable**
  **stock**
20 g (¾ oz) each **coriander**
  and **mint leaves**, finely
  chopped

**Garlic & lemon yogurt**
2 **garlic cloves**, crushed
juice of **1 lemon**
200 ml (7 fl oz) **natural yogurt**
**salt** and **pepper**

**Mix** the harissa paste and oil together in a bowl, add the squash, sweet potato and red peppers, and toss until well coated.

**Spread** the vegetables over a large baking tray and roast in a preheated oven, 200°C (400°F), Gas Mark 6, for 20 minutes until softened and the edges of the vegetables are starting to char.

**Meanwhile,** put the bulgur wheat in a large bowl and pour over the hot stock, then cover and leave to absorb the liquid for 15 minutes until the grains are tender but still have a little bite.

**In** a separate bowl, mix the garlic and lemon juice into the yogurt and season to taste.

**Leave** the bulgur wheat to cool slightly, then toss in the roasted vegetables with the chopped coriander and mint. Serve warm with the garlic and lemon yogurt.

**For superfast harissa and roasted veg soup**, place the roasted vegetables from the recipe above in a blender with 500 ml (17 fl oz) hot vegetable stock, 1 tablespoon harissa paste and 3 tablespoons each of chopped coriander and mint. Blend until smooth and serve in warmed bowls with a dollop of natural yogurt.

# watermelon, olive, green bean & feta salad

Serves **4**
Preparation time **20 minutes**
Cooking time **5 minutes**

300 g (10 oz) **green beans**, halved
1 **red onion**
juice of 2 **limes**
1.5 kg (3 lb) **watermelon**, ripe and sweet
250 g (8 oz) **feta cheese**
100 g (3½ oz) **black olives**, pitted
1 bunch of **flat leaf parsley**, roughly chopped
1 bunch of **mint leaves**, roughly chopped
75 ml (3 fl oz) **extra virgin olive oil**
**salt** and **pepper**

**Blanch** the green beans in a saucepan of boiling water for 3 minutes. Drain, refresh under cold water and set aside.

**Halve** the red onion and cut into thin slices. Place in a small bowl with the drained beans and the lime juice and allow the flavours to meld. Season with salt.

**Meanwhile**, remove the rind and pips from the watermelon and cut into bite-sized pieces. Cut the feta into similarly sized pieces and put them both into a large, wide, shallow bowl or serving dish.

**Add** the red onions and beans, along with their juices, to the wide bowl or serving dish. Scatter over the olives and herbs.

**Season** well with salt and pepper, drizzle with oil and serve at room temperature.

**For Moroccan orange & black olive salad with feta**, peel and segment 4 large oranges (saving any juices) and place them on a serving platter with 100 g (3½ oz) pitted black olives and 250 g (8 oz) cubed feta cheese. Drizzle over 50 ml (2 fl oz) olive oil and scatter over 2 teaspoons of Moroccan spice mix. Season, toss to mix well and scatter over a small handful of mint leaves to serve.

# delicatessen pasta salad

Serves **4**
Preparation time **10 minutes**
Cooking time **5 minutes**

2 × 300 g (10 oz) packs
  **fresh spinach** and **ricotta
  tortellini**
1 × 275 g (9 oz) jar **mixed
  peppers in oil** (from a jar)
1 × 275 g (9 oz) jar
  **mushrooms in olive oil**,
  drained
200 g (7 oz) **Sunblush
  tomatoes**, drained
25 g (1 oz) **basil leaves**
50 g (2 oz) **rocket leaves**
**pepper**

**Bring** a large pan of lightly salted water to the boil.
Add the tortellini and cook according to the packet
instructions. Drain well and tip into a large bowl.

**Add** the jar of mixed peppers, including the oil, along
with the drained mushrooms and Sunblush tomatoes.

**Add** the basil leaves and rocket. Season with black
pepper, stir gently to combine and serve warm.

**For tortellini pasta bake**, cook 2 × 300 g (10 oz) packs
fresh spinach and ricotta tortellini, drain and mix together
in a shallow ovenproof dish with 200 g (7 oz) roasted
mixed peppers, 200 g (7 oz) Sunblush tomatoes and
25 g (1 oz) chopped basil leaves. Whisk together 2 eggs,
200 ml (7 fl oz) double cream and 50 g (2 oz) grated
Parmesan-style vegetarian cheese. Season and pour over
the tortellini mixture. Bake in a preheated oven, 200°C
(400°F), Gas Mark 6, for 15–20 minutes or until bubbling
and golden. Serve warm with a rocket salad.

# fattoush salad

Serves **4**
Preparation time **15 minutes**

1 **pitta bread**, torn into small
  pieces
6 **plum tomatoes**, deseeded
  and roughly chopped
½ **cucumber**, peeled and
  roughly chopped
10 **radishes**, sliced
1 **red onion**, roughly chopped
1 small **Little Gem lettuce**,
  leaves separated
small handful of **mint leaves**

**Lemon & sumac dressing**
200 ml (7 fl oz) **olive oil**
juice of 3 **lemons**
1 **garlic clove**, crushed
2 teaspoons **sumac (or
  ½ teaspoon ground cumin)**
**salt** and **pepper**

**First** make the lemon and sumac dressing. Whisk the olive oil, lemon juice, garlic and sumac together in a bowl. Season to taste.

**To** make the salad, combine the pitta pieces, tomatoes, cucumber, radishes, red onion, lettuce leaves and mint leaves in a large bowl.

**When** ready to serve, pour the dressing over the salad and gently mix together to coat the salad evenly.

### For toasted pitta, hummus and salad 'pizzettas',
finely dice 4 plum tomatoes, ½ cucumber, 6 radishes and ½ red onion and place in a bowl with 1 crushed garlic clove, 50 ml (2 fl oz) olive oil, 2 teaspoons sumac and the juice of 1 lemon. Season and stir to mix well. Allow to stand for 15 minutes. Meanwhile, toast 8 pitta breads until lightly golden and place onto 4 serving plates. Spread 2 tablespoons hummus over each one and top with the prepared salad. Scatter over chopped mint leaves and serve.

# kachumber & basmati rice salad

Serves **4**
Preparation time **15 minutes**
Standing time **5−6 minutes**

1 **red onion**, finely chopped
6 **ripe tomatoes**, finely
  chopped
1 **cucumber**, finely chopped
1 **fresh red chilli**, deseeded
  and finely chopped
small handful of finely chopped
  **coriander**
small handful of finely chopped
  **mint**
400 g (13 oz) **basmati rice**,
  cooked and cooled
juice of 2 large **limes**
2 tablespoons roughly
  chopped **roasted peanuts**
**salt** and **pepper**

**Put** the onion, tomatoes, cucumber, chilli, coriander, mint and rice in a bowl, and pour over the lime juice.

**Season** well, cover and allow to stand at room temperature for 5−6 minutes.

**Before** serving, stir to mix well and scatter over the chopped nuts.

**For linguini with a fresh tomato, chilli and herb sauce**, cook 375 g (12 oz) linguini according to the packet instructions. Meanwhile finely chop 1 red onion, 6 plum tomatoes, 1 red chilli and a small handful coriander and mint leaves. Place in a bowl with 75 ml (3 fl oz) olive oil, season and stir to mix well. When the pasta is cooked, drain and divide among 4 serving plates. Top with the pasta sauce and serve immediately.

# couscous salad with peppers & preserved lemon

Serves **4**
Preparation time **15 minutes**
Cooking time **10–12 minutes**

200 g (7 oz) **giant couscous**
750 ml (1½ pints) hot
  **vegetable stock**
2 **garlic cloves**, crushed
½ teaspoon finely grated
  **fresh root ginger**
1 teaspoon **ground cumin**
¼ teaspoon **ground
  cinnamon**
1 tablespoon **orange zest**
100 g (3½ oz) **pumpkin
  seeds**
50 ml (2 fl oz) **olive oil**
1 **red pepper** and 1 **yellow
  pepper**, deseeded and finely
  chopped
4 **spring onions**, finely sliced
100 g (3½ oz) **cherry
  tomatoes**, quartered
1 tablespoon **preserved
  lemon**, finely chopped
juice of 1 large **orange**
2 tablespoons each finely
  chopped **coriander** and **mint
  leaves**

**Place** the couscous in a saucepan with the stock, garlic, ginger, cumin, cinnamon and orange zest. Bring to the boil and simmer for 10–12 minutes or until the couscous is tender.

**Meanwhile,** toast the pumpkin seeds in a dry frying pan.

**Drain** the couscous and place in a large mixing bowl with the olive oil, peppers, spring onions, tomatoes and preserved lemon.

**Add** the orange juice, chopped herbs and pumpkin seeds. Toss gently to mix well and serve immediately.

**For mixed pepper tagine**, heat 3 tablespoons olive oil in a saucepan and add 4 chopped spring onions, 2 chopped garlic cloves, 1 teaspoon grated fresh root ginger, 1 teaspoon ground cumin, ¼ teaspoon ground cinnamon and 2 deseeded and chopped peppers (1 red and 1 yellow). Stir-fry for 2–3 minutes, then pour over 500 ml (17 fl oz) hot vegetable stock. Bring to the boil and simmer for 10–12 minutes, then add 1 tablespoon chopped preserved lemon. Mix together 1 tablespoon cornflour with 2 tablespoons cold water, add to the tagine, stir and cook until thickened slightly. Remove from the heat and garnish with chopped coriander before serving with couscous or rice.

# lentil, mushroom & peppadew pepper salad

Serves **4**
Preparation time **15 minutes**
Cooking time **5 minutes**

50 ml (2 fl oz) **olive oil**
300 g (10 oz) **button mushrooms**, halved or quartered
2 tablespoons **cider vinegar**
1 tablespoon **Dijon mustard**
200 g (7 oz) **mild Peppadew peppers**, drained and roughly chopped
6 **spring onions**, finely sliced
1 × 400 g (13 oz) can **green lentils**, drained and rinsed
3 **Little Gem lettuces**, leaves separated
100 g (3½ oz) **vegetarian goats' cheese**
**black pepper**

**Heat** 2 tablespoons of the oil in a nonstick frying pan. Add the mushrooms and fry over a high heat until just starting to soften.

**Remove** from the heat, then stir in the remaining oil with the vinegar and mustard. Stir well until mixed, then add the Peppadew peppers, spring onions and lentils and mix well again.

**Arrange** the lettuce leaves over 4 plates. Spoon the lentil salad over the top, crumble over the goats' cheese and serve seasoned with freshly ground black pepper.

**For spiced mushroom and lentil curry**, heat 2 tablespoons olive oil in a saucepan and fry 6 chopped spring onions, 2 chopped garlic cloves and 1 teaspoon finely chopped fresh root ginger for 2–3 minutes over a low heat. Add 2 teaspoons cumin seeds, 1 teaspoon black mustard seeds and 2 tablespoons mild curry powder and stir-fry for 1–2 minutes. Stir in 400 g (13 oz) sliced button mushrooms and stir-fry over a high heat for 3–4 minutes. Add 1 × 400 g (13 oz) canned green lentils, 200 g (7 oz) chopped tomatoes and 200 ml (7 fl oz) vegetable stock. Bring to the boil and simmer gently for 15–20 minutes. Remove from the heat, stir in 65 g (2½ oz) crème fraîche, season and serve with rice or warmed naan breads.

# grilled halloumi, mixed peppers & rocket salad

Serves **4**
Preparation time **10 minutes**
Cooking time **4–6 minutes**

24 **vine-ripened cherry tomatoes**
200 g (7 oz) **mixed peppers in oil** (from a jar), drained and sliced
100 g (3½ oz) **rocket leaves**
2 × 200 g (7 oz) packs **halloumi**, sliced

**Parsley & caper dressing**
grated zest of ½ **lemon** and juice from 1 **lemon**
75 ml (3 fl oz) **olive oil**
handful of **flat leaf parsley**, chopped
2 tablespoons small **capers**, drained and rinsed
**pepper**

**First** make the parsley and caper dressing. Whisk together the lemon zest and juice, olive oil, parsley, capers and black pepper, then set aside.

**Halve** the tomatoes and divide among 4 plates, along with the peppers and rocket.

**Place** the slices of halloumi on a preheated griddle pan and place under a preheated medium grill. Cook for 2–3 minutes on each side until just beginning to warm and soften.

**Transfer** the warm halloumi to the plates, drizzle with the dressing and serve immediately.

**For grilled halloumi wraps**, in a large bowl, mix together 2 tablespoons capers, 300 g (10 oz) halved cherry tomatoes, 200 g (7 oz) chopped roasted mixed peppers (from a jar) and 40 g (1½ oz) chopped rocket leaves. Squeeze over the juice of 1 lime and season well. Meanwhile, warm 200 g (7 oz) sliced halloumi and 4 large flatbread wraps in a preheated oven, 150°C (300°F), Gas Mark 2. To serve, divide the vegetable mixture and halloumi among the 4 wraps and fold over to enclose the filling.

# quick curried egg salad

Serves **4**
Preparation time **10 minutes**

8 hard-boiled **eggs**
4 **tomatoes**, cut into wedges
2 **Little Gem lettuces**, leaves
  separated
¼ **cucumber**, sliced
**thyme leaves**, to garnish

**Curry dressing**
200 ml (7 fl oz) **natural yogurt**
1 tablespoon **mild curry
  powder**
3 tablespoons **tomato purée**
juice of 2 **limes**
75 g (3 oz) **mayonnaise**
**salt** and **pepper**

**Shell** the eggs, halve them and place on a large platter with the tomatoes, lettuce leaves and cucumber.

**For** the dressing, mix the yogurt together with the curry powder, tomato purée, lime juice and mayonnaise.

**Season** the dressing, then pour it over the salad. Serve immediately, garnished with thyme leaves.

**For egg & tomato curry**, heat 2 tablespoons sunflower oil in a large, nonstick wok or frying pan. Add 1 tablespoon cumin seeds, 1 tablespoon black mustard seeds, 2 crushed garlic cloves, 2 dried red chillies and 10 curry leaves and stir-fry for 30–40 seconds. Add 1 halved and thinly sliced onion and 2 tablespoons curry powder and stir in 200 g (7 oz) canned chopped tomatoes, 1 teaspoon sugar and 200 ml (7 fl oz) coconut cream. Bring to the boil, reduce the heat to medium–low and cook for 8–10 minutes, stirring often. Add 8 shelled hard-boiled eggs and cook for 10–12 minutes until the sauce is thickened. Season with salt, garnish with coriander leaves and serve with warm naan bread.

# quinoa, courgette & pomegranate salad

Serves **4**
Preparation time **15 minutes**
Cooking time **20 minutes**

75 g (3 oz) **quinoa**
1 large **courgette**
2 tablespoons **olive oil**
4 **spring onions**, finely sliced
100 g (3½ oz) **cherry tomatoes**, halved
1 **red chilli**, finely chopped
100 g (3½ oz) **pomegranate seeds** (or seeds of ½ **pomegranate**)
small handful of finely chopped **flat leaf parsley**

**Dressing**
1 tablespoon **white wine vinegar**
2 tablespoons **olive oil**
**salt** and **pepper**

**Cook** the quinoa following the packet instructions, then drain and rinse under cold water. Drain again.

**Meanwhile**, cut the ends off the courgette, then cut it into ribbons using a vegetable peeler and place into a large bowl.

**For** the dressing, whisk together the vinegar and oil, then season with salt and pepper.

**Add** the rest of the ingredients to the large bowl. Pour over the dressing, toss everything together and serve.

**For warm grilled courgette and aubergine salad with quinoa**, cook 50 g (2 oz) quinoa according to the packet instructions. Meanwhile, slice 2 large courgettes, and 1 aubergine into 1 cm (½ in) slices, brush with a little olive oil and cook in batches in a griddle pan over a high heat for 4–5 minutes on each side or until tender. Place in a wide bowl and scatter over 4 finely sliced spring onions, 100 g (3½ oz) halved cherry tomatoes and the cooked quinoa. Drizzle with a mixture of 50 ml (2 fl oz) olive oil and 1 tablespoon white wine vinegar. Season, scatter with mint leaves and serve.

# roasted vegetable couscous salad

Serves **4**
Preparation time **20 minutes**
Cooking time **15–20 minutes**

1 **red** and 1 **yellow pepper**,
   deseeded and cut into
   2.5 cm (1 in) pieces
1 medium **aubergine**, cut into
   2.5 cm (1 in) pieces
1 **courgette**, cut into 2.5 cm
   (1 in) cubes
2 small **red onions**, peeled
   and cut into thick wedges
**olive oil**, to drizzle
200 g (7 oz) **couscous**
6–8 **preserved lemons**, halved
large handful of chopped **mint**
   and **coriander leaves**
50 g (2 oz) **pine nuts**, toasted
150 g (5 oz) **vegetarian feta
   cheese**, crumbled
100 g (3½ oz) **pomegranate
   seeds**
**salt** and **pepper**

**Orange dressing**
juice of **1 orange**
75 ml (3 fl oz) **olive oil**
1 teaspoon **ground cumin**
½ teaspoon **ground cinnamon**
**salt** and **pepper**

**Place** the vegetables on a large nonstick baking tray. Drizzle with a little olive oil and season well. Roast in a preheated oven, 200°C (400°F), Gas Mark 6, for 15–20 minutes, or until the edges of the vegetables are just starting to char.

**Meanwhile,** put the couscous in a wide bowl and pour over boiling hot water to just cover. Season well. Cover with clingfilm and allow to stand, undisturbed, for 10 minutes or until all the liquid has been absorbed. Fluff up the grains with a fork and place on a wide, shallow serving platter.

**Make** the dressing by mixing together the orange juice, olive oil, cumin and cinnamon and season well.

**Fold** the roasted vegetables, preserved lemons and herbs into the couscous, pour over the dressing and toss to mix well.

**Just** before serving, scatter over the pine nuts, feta and pomegranate seeds and serve immediately.

**For lemon and herb couscous**, tip 500 g (1 lb) cooked couscous into a large bowl with 20 g (¾ oz) each chopped mint and coriander, 6 sliced spring onions and 6 chopped preserved lemons. Season, toss to mix well and serve, garnished with toasted pine nuts.

# midweek meals

# black-eyed bean & red pepper stew

Serves **4**
Preparation time **15 minutes**
Cooking time **20–25 minutes**

2 tablespoons **olive oil**
4 **shallots**, finely chopped
2 **garlic cloves**, crushed
2 **celery stalks**, diced
1 large **carrot**, peeled and cut into 1 cm (½ in) pieces
1 **red pepper**, deseeded and cut into 1 cm (½ in) pieces
1 teaspoon **dried mixed herbs**
2 teaspoons **ground cumin**
1 teaspoon **ground cinnamon**
2 × 400 g (13 oz) cans **tomatoes**
2 tablespoons **sun-dried tomato purée**
75 ml (3 fl oz) **vegetable stock**
2 × 400 g (13 oz) cans **black-eyed beans** in water, drained
15 g (1 oz) **coriander leaves**, finely chopped, plus extra to garnish
**salt** and **pepper**
cooked **basmati rice**, to serve

**Heat** the oil in a large frying pan over a high heat.

**Add** the shallots, garlic, celery, carrot and red pepper and stir-fry for 2–3 minutes or until lightly starting to colour.

**Add** the dried herbs, cumin, cinnamon, tomatoes, tomato purée and stock and bring to the boil. Reduce the heat to medium, cover and cook gently for 12–15 minutes or until the vegetables are tender, breaking up the tomatoes into small pieces with a wooden spoon towards the end of the cooking time.

**Stir** in the black-eyed beans and cook for 2–3 minutes or until piping hot.

**Season** well, remove from the heat and scatter over the chopped coriander. Garnish with coriander leaves and serve with basmati rice.

**For black-eyed bean & vegetable salad**, finely chop 2 carrots, 2 celery stalks, 1 red pepper, 2 tomatoes and 2 shallots and place in a bowl with 50 ml (2 fl oz) olive oil and the juice of 2 limes. Season and add 1 × 400 g (13 oz) can black-eyed beans, drained, and a large handful of chopped coriander and mint leaves. Toss to mix well and serve with warm flatbreads.

# rustic italian-style mushrooms with soft polenta

Serves **4**
Preparation time **10 minutes**
Cooking time **10–15 minutes**

150 g (5 oz) **polenta**
1 tablespoon finely chopped
    **rosemary leaves**
1 tablespoon finely chopped
    **sage leaves**
20 g (¾ oz) **flat leaf parsley**,
    finely chopped
125 g (4 oz) **butter**
1.5 litres (2½ pints) hot
    **vegetable stock**
750 g (1½ lb) large
    **Portobello mushrooms**,
    thickly sliced
3 **garlic cloves**, crushed
125 g (4 oz) **soft cheese with
    garlic and herbs**
½ teaspoon **red chilli flakes**
**salt** and **pepper**

**Place** the polenta, rosemary, sage, half the parsley and half the butter in a saucepan over a medium heat and gradually whisk in the stock, stirring continuously.

**Reduce** the heat to low, season well and stir constantly until the polenta becomes very thick and starts bubbling (this will take 6–8 minutes). Remove from the heat and keep warm.

**Meanwhile,** heat the remaining butter in a large nonstick frying pan over a high heat. Add the mushrooms and garlic and stir-fry for 6–8 minutes. Season well and stir in the soft cheese and chilli flakes. Stir-fry for 2–3 minutes until bubbling. Remove from the heat and stir in the remaining parsley.

**Serve** immediately on warmed plates over the polenta.

**For creamy mushroom & herb pasta**, cook 375 g (12 oz) quick-cook pasta according to the packet instructions. Meanwhile, heat a large frying pan over a high heat and add 2 tablespoons butter, 2 finely chopped garlic cloves and 750 g (1½ lb) thinly sliced Portobello mushrooms. Stir-fry over a high heat for 3–4 minutes and then stir in 200 g (7 oz) soft cheese with garlic and herbs. Season, toss to mix well and stir in 3 tablespoons chopped parsley. Serve over the pasta.

# creamy courgette orzo pasta

Serves **4**

Preparation time **15 minutes**

Cooking time **15–20 minutes**

375 g (12 oz) **dried orzo**
(rice-shaped pasta)

1 tablespoon **butter**

1 tablespoon **olive oil**

1 **red chilli**, deseeded and
finely chopped

2 **garlic cloves**, finely chopped

4 **spring onions**, very finely
chopped

3 medium **courgettes**,
coarsely grated

finely grated zest of 1 small
**lemon**

150 g (5 oz) **soft cheese with
garlic and herbs**

15 g (½ oz) **flat leaf parsley**,
finely chopped

**salt** and **pepper**

**Bring** a large pan of lightly salted water to the boil, then
cook the pasta according to the packet instructions.

**Meanwhile,** heat the butter and olive oil in a large frying
pan, then add the chilli, garlic, spring onions
and courgettes. Cook over a medium-low heat for
10–15 minutes, or until softened, stirring often.

**Reduce** the heat and add the lemon zest. Cook gently
for 3–4 minutes, add the soft cheese and mix thoroughly.
Season to taste.

**Drain** the pasta and add to the courgette mixture.
Stir in the parsley, mix well and serve immediately.

### For minted courgette, cherry tomato & orzo pasta
**salad**, cook 375 g (12 oz) dried orzo pasta according
to the packet instructions. Meanwhile, place 2 coarsely
grated courgettes, 4 sliced spring onions, 15 g (½ oz)
finely chopped mint leaves and 200 g (7 oz) halved
cherry tomatoes in a wide salad bowl. Make a dressing by
whisking together 1 finely chopped red chilli, 2 crushed
garlic cloves, 75 ml (3 fl oz) olive oil, the juice of 1 lemon
and 1 teaspoon clear honey. Season well. Drain the
pasta and rinse under cold running water until cool. Drain
again and add to the salad bowl. Pour over the dressing
and toss to mix well before serving.

# greek-style summer omelette

Serves **4**
Preparation time **20 minutes**
Cooking time **15–20 minutes**

8 large **eggs**
1 teaspoon dried **oregano**
1 tablespoon finely chopped **mint**
15 g (½ oz) **flat leaf parsley**, finely chopped
2 tablespoons **olive oil**
2 small **red onions**, peeled and roughly chopped
2 large **ripe tomatoes**, roughly chopped
½ **courgette**, roughly chopped
100 g (3½ oz) **black olives**, pitted
100 g (3½ oz) **vegetarian feta cheese**, roughly cubed
**salt** and **pepper**
**crisp green salad**, to serve

**Whisk** the eggs in a bowl and add the oregano, mint and parsley. Season well.

**Heat** the oil in a large nonstick frying pan. Add the red onion and fry over a high heat for 3–4 minutes or until coloured around the edges.

**Add** the tomatoes, courgette and olives and cook for 3–4 minutes or until the vegetables begin to soften.

**Meanwhile,** preheat the grill to medium-high.

**Reduce** the heat to medium and pour the eggs into the frying pan. Cook for 3–4 minutes, stirring as they begin to set, until they are firm but still slightly runny in places.

**Scatter** over the feta, then place the pan under the preheated grill for 4–5 minutes or until the omelette is puffed up and golden.

**Cut** into wedges and serve with a crisp green salad, if liked.

**For a classic Greek salad**, thinly slice 2 red onions, 4 tomatoes and 1 cucumber and place in a wide salad bowl with 200 g (7 oz) cubed feta cheese and 100 g (3½ oz) pitted black olives. Drizzle over 75 ml (3 fl oz) olive oil and scatter over 1 teaspoon dried oregano. Season, toss to mix well and serve.

# spinach, cherry tomato & blue cheese pasta salad

Serves **4**
Preparation time **10 minutes**

400 g (13 oz) cooked and
    cooled **macaroni** (or any
    short-shaped pasta)
50 g (2 oz) **baby spinach**
400 g (13 oz) **cherry
    tomatoes**, halved
4 **spring onions**, sliced
200 ml (7 fl oz) ready-made
    **vegetarian blue cheese
    dressing**
**salt** and **pepper**

**Place** the cooked and cooled macaroni in a salad bowl
with the spinach, cherry tomatoes and spring onions.

**Drizzle** over the blue cheese dressing.

**Season** to taste, toss to mix well and serve immediately.

**For macaroni cheese with spinach & tomatoes**, cook
275 g (9 oz) dried macaroni in a large saucepan of boiling
salted water for 8–10 minutes, drain well and set aside.
Meanwhile, melt 40 g (1 ½ oz) butter over a medium heat
in a heavy-based saucepan. Add 40 g (1 ½ oz) plain flour
and stir to form a roux, cooking for a few minutes. Warm
600 ml (1 pint) milk separately. Whisk the warmed milk
into the roux, a little at a time. Cook for 10–15 minutes
until the sauce is thick and smooth. Stir in 100 g (3 ½ oz)
finely chopped baby spinach leaves and 100 g (3 ½ oz)
cherry tomatoes and season well. Remove from the heat,
add 200 g (7 oz) vegetarian Cheddar cheese and stir
until the cheese is well combined and melted. Add the
macaroni and mix well. Transfer to a deep ovenproof dish.
Scatter over 50 g (2 oz) vegetarian Cheddar cheese and
place under a preheated hot grill. Cook until the cheese is
browned and bubbling. Serve immediately.

# mixed bean kedgeree

Serves **4**
Preparation time **10 minutes**
Cooking time **15–20 minutes**

4 **eggs**
2 tablespoons **olive oil**
1 **onion**, chopped
2 tablespoons **mild curry powder**
250 g (8 oz) **long grain rice**
750 ml (1 ¼ pints) **vegetable stock**
2 × 400 g (13 oz) cans **mixed beans**, drained and rinsed
150 ml (¼ pint) **soured cream**

**To garnish**
2 **tomatoes**, finely chopped
3 tablespoons chopped **herbs**

**Hard** boil the eggs, then plunge into cold water to cool. Shell, cut into wedges and set aside.

**Meanwhile,** heat the oil in a saucepan and fry the onion for 3–4 minutes, until soft.

**Stir** in the curry powder and rice, then add the stock. Bring to the boil, cover and simmer for 10–15 minutes until the rice is cooked.

**Stir** through the beans and soured cream. Season to taste and serve topped with the eggs and garnish with the tomatoes and herbs.

**For spiced bean & rice broth**, heat 1 tablespoon olive oil in a saucepan and add 1 chopped onion and 1 tablespoon curry powder and stir-fry for 1–2 minutes. Stir in 1 litre (1¾ pints) hot vegetable stock, 2 × 400 g (13 oz) cans mixed beans, 2 chopped tomatoes and 75 g (3 oz) long grain rice. Bring to the boil and cook, uncovered, for 15 minutes or until the rice is tender. Season, stir in 15 g (½ oz) chopped coriander and serve ladled into warmed bowls.

# kale & parmesan pesto linguini

Serves **4**
Preparation time **10 minutes**
Cooking time **10–12 minutes**

375 g (12 oz) **dried linguini**

**Kale & parmesan pesto**
300 g (10 oz) **kale**
2 tablespoons **olive oil**
3 **garlic cloves**, crushed
100 g (3½ oz) **toasted pine nuts**
100 g (3½ oz) **mascarpone cheese**
100 g (3½ oz) **Parmesan-style vegetarian cheese**, grated, plus extra shavings to garnish
½ teaspoon grated **nutmeg**
**salt** and **pepper**

**Cook** the pasta according to the packet instructions.

**Meanwhile,** wash the kale well, remove any tough stalks and chop roughly.

**Heat** the oil in a large saucepan and sauté the garlic for 2–3 minutes. Add the kale to the pan. Cover and cook for 2–3 minutes, or until the kale starts to wilt.

**Place** the pine nuts into a food processor or blender and whizz until smooth. Tip in the mascarpone, Parmesan and nutmeg. Whizz again.

**Add** the kale and garlic mixture and whizz until smooth. Season to taste.

**Drain** the pasta and return it to the pan. Add the pesto and toss to mix well. Serve garnished with shavings of pecorino.

**For tomato & pesto soup**, heat 2 × 400 g (13 oz) cans cream of tomato soup until piping hot and ladle into shallow soup plates. Swirl 65 g (2½ oz) Kale and Parmesan Pesto (from the recipe above) into each serving and scatter over 100 g (3½ oz) ready-made croutons and serve immediately.

# ranch-style eggs

Serves **4**
Preparation time **10 minutes**
Cooking time **15 minutes**

2 tablespoons **olive oil**
1 **onion**, finely sliced
1 **red chilli**, deseeded and
  finely chopped
1 **garlic clove**, crushed
1 teaspoon **ground cumin**
1 teaspoon dried **oregano**
1 × 400 g (13 oz) can **cherry
  tomatoes**
200 g (7 oz) **mixed peppers
  in oil** (from a jar), drained
  and roughly chopped
4 **eggs**
**salt** and **pepper**
15 g (½ oz) **coriander**, finely
  chopped, to garnish

**Heat** the oil in a large frying pan and add the onion, chilli, garlic, cumin and oregano.

**Fry** gently for about 5 minutes or until soft, then add the tomatoes and peppers and cook for a further 5 minutes. If the sauce looks dry, add a splash of water.

**Season** well and make 4 hollows in the mixture, break an egg into each and cover the pan. Cook for 5 minutes or until the eggs are just set.

**Serve** immediately, garnished with chopped coriander.

**For spicy Mexican-style scrambled eggs**, heat 1 tablespoon each olive oil and butter in a large frying pan. Whisk together 8 eggs with 1 crushed garlic clove, 1 finely chopped red chilli, 1 teaspoon dried oregano and 1 teaspoon ground cumin. Season, pour into the frying pan and cook over a medium-low heat, stirring often or until the eggs are scrambled and cooked to your liking. Serve with warm tortillas and garnish with chopped coriander.

# rigatoni with fresh tomato, chilli, garlic & basil

Serves **4**
Preparation time **15 minutes**
Cooking time **10–15 minutes**

6 large **ripe plum tomatoes**
1 tablespoon **extra-virgin olive oil**
2 cloves **garlic**, finely diced
1 **red chilli**, deseeded and finely diced
75 ml (3 fl oz) **vegetable stock**
25 g (1 oz) **basil leaves**, finely chopped
375 g (12 oz) **dried rigatoni**
grated **Parmesan-style vegetarian cheese**, to serve (optional)
**salt** and **pepper**

**Place** the tomatoes in a bowl and pour over boiling water to cover. Leave for 1–2 minutes, then drain, cut across the stalk end of each tomato and peel off the skins.

**When** cool enough to handle, cut the tomatoes in half horizontally and shake or gently spoon out the seeds, then finely dice the flesh.

**Heat** the oil in a large, nonstick frying pan and add the garlic and chilli. Cook on a medium-low heat for 1–2 minutes or until the garlic is fragrant but not coloured.

**Add** the tomatoes, stock and basil, season well and cook gently for 6–8 minutes or until thickened, stirring often.

**Meanwhile,** cook the rigatoni according to the packet instructions, drain and toss into the tomato sauce.

**Spoon** into warmed bowls and serve with grated Parmesan, if desired.

**For no-cook fresh tomato, chilli & basil sauce**, finely chop 6 ripe plum tomatoes and place in a bowl with 2 crushed garlic cloves, 1 finely chopped red chilli and 50 g (2 oz) finely chopped basil leaves. Pour over 125 ml (4 fl oz) extra virgin olive oil and season well. Serve over cooked pasta, couscous or rice.

# pasta with asparagus, beans & pesto

Serves **4**
Preparation time **10 minutes**
Cooking time **9–12 minutes**

400 g (13 oz) **dried short-shaped pasta**
200 g (7 oz) **asparagus tips**, halved
200 g (7 oz) **fine green beans**, halved
2 tablespoons **olive oil**
2 tablespoons **fresh** or **ready-made breadcrumbs**
100 g (3½ oz) **crème fraîche**
100 g (3½ oz) **ready-made vegetarian pesto**
25 g (1 oz) **Parmesan-style vegetarian cheese**, grated
**salt** and **pepper**

**Bring** a large pan of salted water to the boil. Add the pasta and cook according to the packet instructions, adding the asparagus and beans for the last 2 minutes of the cooking time.

**Meanwhile,** heat the oil in a small frying pan and fry the breadcrumbs with a pinch of salt until golden.

**Drain** the pasta and vegetables, then return to the pan along with the crème fraiche, pesto and a generous grinding of pepper.

**Serve** in warmed bowls, scattered with the crispy breadcrumbs and freshly grated Parmesan.

**For asparagus & green bean risotto with pesto**, heat 2 tablespoons each olive oil and butter in a heavy-based saucepan. When the butter is foaming, add 1 chopped onion and 2 chopped garlic cloves and cook for 2–3 minutes, until beginning to soften. Add 375 g (12 oz) risotto rice, 200 g (7 oz) asparagus tips and 200 g (7 oz) halved green beans. Stir well and cook for a 1–2 minutes then add 150 ml (5 fl oz) dry white wine and simmer for 1 minute, stirring continuously. Reduce the heat and ladle in 1.2 litres (2 pints) hot vegetable stock, 1 ladleful at a time, stirring continuously until each amount is absorbed and the rice is creamy but still firm to the bite. Remove from the heat and stir in 50 g (2 oz) grated Parmesan-style vegetarian cheese and 65 g (2½ oz) vegetarian pesto. Season well and serve immediately.

# stir-fried vegetable rice

Serves **4**
Preparation time **10 minutes**
Cooking time **10–15 minutes**

2 tablespoons **sunflower oil**

6 **spring onions**, cut
   diagonally into 2.5 cm
   (1 in) lengths

2 **garlic cloves**, crushed

1 teaspoon finely grated **fresh
   root ginger**

1 **red pepper**, deseeded and
   finely chopped

1 **carrot**, peeled and finely
   diced

300 g (10 oz) **peas**

500 g (1 lb) cooked, **white
   long grain rice**

1 tablespoon **dark soy sauce**

1 tablespoon **sweet chilli
   sauce**

chopped **coriander** and **mint**,
   to serve

**Heat** the oil in a large, nonstick wok and add the spring onions, garlic and ginger. Stir-fry for 4–5 minutes and then add the red pepper, carrot and peas. Stir-fry over a high heat for 3–4 minutes.

**Stir** in the rice, soy sauce and sweet chilli sauce and stir-fry for 3–4 minutes or until the rice is heated through and piping hot.

**Remove** from the heat and serve immediately, garnished with the chopped herbs.

**For veggie noodle stir-fry**, heat 2 tablespoons oil in a wok and add a 300 g (10 oz) pack of prepared stir-fry vegetables. Stir-fry for 2–3 minutes over a high heat and then add 2 × 300 g (10 oz) packs fresh egg noodles and 1 × 125 g (4 oz) sachet ready-made vegetarian stir-fry sauce. Stir-fry for 1–2 minutes or until piping hot and serve immediately.

# tomato & aubergine pappardelle

Serves **4**
Preparation time **15 minutes**
Cooking time **15–20 minutes**

50 ml (2 fl oz) **extra virgin olive oil**
1 large **aubergine**, cut into 1.5 cm (¾ in) dice
1 small **onion**, finely diced
2 **garlic cloves**, crushed
1 × 350 g (11½ oz) jar **tomato and basil pasta sauce**
375 g (12 oz) dried **pappardelle** or **tagliatelle**
250 g (8 oz) **vegetarian mozzarella cheese**, drained and diced

**To garnish**
25 g (1 oz) **Parmesan-style vegetarian cheese**, grated (optional)
**basil leaves**, to garnish (optional)

**Put** a large pan of salted water on to boil.

**Heat** the oil in a large frying pan over a medium-high heat. Add the aubergine and onion and cook, stirring, for 5 minutes.

**Add** the garlic and cook for 1 minute. Add the tomato sauce and 200 ml (7 fl oz) water to the pan, bring to a simmer and cook for 8–10 minutes, or until the aubergines are just tender. Season to taste.

**Meanwhile,** cook the pasta according to the packet instructions. Remove from the heat, drain and return to the pan.

**Stir** the mozzarella into the sauce until it begins to melt and becomes stringy, then add to the pasta. Toss to mix well, scatter over the Parmesan and garnish with basil leaves, if desired.

**For tomato, aubergine & mozzarella pizzas**, preheat the oven to 220°C (425°F), Gas Mark 7. Place 2 ready-made pizza bases on 2 baking sheets and spread over the tomato and aubergine sauce from the above recipe. Scatter over 250 g (8 oz) diced mozzarella and place in the oven for 8–10 minutes. Serve immediately.

# tex-mex sweetcorn salad

Serves **4**
Preparation time **10 minutes**

400 g (13 oz) **sweetcorn
  kernels**
400 g (13 oz) **mixed peppers
  in oil** (from a jar), drained
  and sliced
1 **red onion**, finely chopped
25 g (1 oz) **jalapeño peppers**
  (from a jar), chopped
1 × 400 g (13 oz) can **red
  kidney beans**, drained
15 g (½ oz) **parsley**, chopped
75 ml (3 fl oz) **ready-made
  vegetarian salad dressing**
**salt** and **pepper**

**Place** the sweetcorn kernels in a bowl with the peppers, onion, jalapeño peppers and kidney beans. Scatter over the chopped parsley.

**Drizzle** over the salad dressing, season, toss to mix well and serve immediately.

**For sweetcorn, red pepper and potato hash**, bring a pan of salted water to the boil and cook 400 g (13 oz) diced potatoes for 5 minutes. Drain well. Heat 2 tablespoons each oil and butter in a large, deep frying pan over a medium heat. Add the potatoes and cook for 5–6 minutes, turning once. Add 1 diced red pepper and fry for 2–3 minutes. Add 400 g (13 oz) sweetcorn kernels to the pan and stir in 1 chopped red chilli, 6 sliced spring onions and 2 sliced garlic cloves. Season and cook for 5 minutes until cooked through. Meanwhile, fry 4 eggs until cooked to your liking and serve the hash on warmed plates topped with the eggs.

# smoked cheese, pepper & spinach quesadillas

Serves **4**
Preparation time **20 minutes**
Cooking time **10–12 minutes**

300 g (10 oz) **baby spinach**
200 g (7 oz) **mixed peppers in oil** (from a jar), drained and roughly chopped
8 **spring onions**, trimmed and finely chopped
200 g (7 oz) **smoked vegetarian hard cheese**, finely diced
150 g (5 oz) **mild vegetarian Cheddar cheese**, grated
1 **red chilli**, deseeded and finely chopped
15 g (½ oz) **coriander leaves**, finely chopped
8 **soft corn tortillas**
**salt** and **pepper**
**olive oil**, for greasing
**soured cream**, to serve

**Blanch** the spinach in a large saucepan of lightly salted boiling water for 1–2 minutes. Drain thoroughly through a fine sieve, pressing out all the liquid. Transfer to a bowl with the roasted peppers, spring onions, smoked cheese, Cheddar, chilli and coriander. Season and mix well.

**Scatter** a quarter of the spinach mixture over a tortilla, top with another tortilla and press together. Make a further 3 quesadillas in the same way.

**Grease** 2 large frying pans with a little olive oil and place over a medium heat. Put 1 quesadilla into each pan and cook for 2 minutes until golden. Invert onto a plate, then slide back into the pan and cook for another 2 minutes, until the filling is hot and the cheese is just melting. Set aside and cook 2 more quesadillas.

**Cut** each quesadilla into 4 and serve with soured cream.

**For spicy spinach, pepper and smoked cheese burgers**, heat 2 tablespoons olive oil in a large wok or frying pan and add 6 finely sliced spring onions and 200 g (7 oz) baby spinach. Stir-fry for 5–6 minutes or until the spinach has wilted. Season and set aside. Split 4 burger buns, lightly toast and spread 2 tablespoons of mayonnaise on each half. Divide 200 g (7 oz) drained and sliced roasted peppers (from a jar) among the 4 burger bases and top each with the spinach mixture and 2 slices of smoked cheese. Cover with the 4 toasted bun tops, press down lightly and serve.

# herby bulgur & chickpea salad

Serves **4**
Preparation time **10 minutes**

1 × 400 g (13 oz) **can
  chickpeas**, drained
100 g (3½ oz) cooked **bulgur
  wheat**
200 g (7 oz) **roasted red
  peppers in oil** (from a jar),
  drained and chopped
large handful of chopped **dill**
large handful of chopped
  **coriander**

**Orange & cumin dressing**
75 ml (3 fl oz) **olive oil**
juice of **1 orange**
1 teaspoon **ground cumin**
**salt** and **pepper**

**Place** the chickpeas in a bowl with the bulgur wheat
and peppers. Add the dill and coriander.

**Whisk** together the olive oil, orange juice and cumin
and season well. Pour the dressing over the salad, toss
to mix well and serve immediately.

**For chickpea & bulgur pilaf**, heat 2 tablespoons olive
oil in a large saucepan. Add 1 finely chopped red onion
and fry over a medium-low heat for 10–12 minutes,
stirring often, or until the onion is lightly golden. Stir
in 1 crushed garlic clove, 1 teaspoon ground cumin,
1 teaspoon ground cinnamon and 175 g (6 oz) bulgur
wheat and cook, stirring, for 1–2 minutes to lightly toast
the grains. Pour over 350 ml (12 fl oz) hot vegetable
stock, stir well, then bring to the boil. Cover and reduce
the heat to medium-low and gently simmer for 6–8
minutes or until all the liquid is absorbed. Remove from
the heat and add 200 g (7 oz) roasted red peppers from a
jar (drained and roughly chopped) and 1 × 400 g (13 oz)
can chickpeas (without stirring them in). Cover and allow
to stand for 5–10 minutes. Just before serving, remove
the lid from the pilaf and fluff up the grains with a fork,
mixing in the red pepper and chickpeas. Carefully fold in
25 g (1 oz) each finely chopped dill and flat leaf parsley,
along with 2 tablespoons finely chopped mint leaves.
Finally, scatter over goats' cheese. Season to taste and
serve hot, warm or cold.

# cold summer soba noodle salad

Serves **4**

Preparation time **15 minutes**

625 g (1 ¼ lb) cooked **soba noodles**

2 **carrots**, finely julienned

6 **spring onions**, finely shredded

1 **red pepper**, finely sliced

**Soy dressing**

50 ml (2 fl oz) **dark soy sauce**

3 tablespoons **sesame oil**

1 tablespoon **mirin**

1 tablespoon **caster sugar**

½ teaspoon **chilli oil**

**Place** the soba noodles in a wide bowl with the carrots, spring onions and pepper.

**In** a separate bowl, making a dressing by mixing together the soy sauce, sesame oil, mirin, sugar and chilli oil, then pour over the noodle mixture.

**Toss** to mix well and serve chilled or at room temperature.

**For soba noodle & shiitake mushroom soup**, cook 250 g (8 oz) soba noodles according to the packet instructions. Divide the noodles among 4 serving bowls. Meanwhile, place 1 litre (1 ¾ pints) hot vegetable stock, 3 tablespoons mirin, 200 g sliced shiitake mushrooms and 75 ml (3 fl oz) dark soy sauce in a saucepan and bring to the boil. Add 200 g (7 oz) halved sugarsnap peas and continue to cook for 4–5 minutes, or until the sugarsnaps are cooked. Taste for seasoning, adding more soy sauce if liked. Ladle the broth with some mushrooms and sugarsnaps over the soba noodles in the bowls and scatter with sliced spring onions to serve.

# tortellini, roasted pepper & rocket salad

Serves **4**
Preparation time **10 minutes**
Cooking time **3–5 minutes**

2 × 250 g (8 oz) **ready-made
  fresh spinach** and **ricotta
  tortellini**
400 g (13 oz) **roasted red
  peppers in oil** (from a jar),
  drained
100 g (3½ oz) **rocket leaves**
1 **red onion**, thinly sliced
200 ml (7 fl oz) **fresh Italian-
  style vegetarian salad
  dressing**
**pepper**

**Cook** the tortellini according to the packet instructions.

**Meanwhile** chop the peppers and place in a bowl with the rocket leaves and onion. Add the cooked tortellini.

**Pour** over the salad dressing, toss to mix well and serve seasoned with black pepper.

**For cheesy tortellini and red pepper grill**, preheat the grill to medium-high. Place 2 × 250 g (8 oz) cooked ready-made fresh spinach and ricotta tortellini in a lightly greased shallow ovenproof dish. Stir in 400 g (13 oz) chopped roasted red and yellow peppers in oil (from a jar), drained, and 1 × 400 g (13 oz) can chopped tomatoes with garlic and herbs, and toss to mix well. Season and pour over a 350 g (11½ oz) tub ready-made fresh cheese sauce to cover. Place under the grill for 4–5 minutes or until the top is golden and bubbling. Serve warm with a rocket salad.

# creamy mushroom & herb pancakes

Serves **4**
Preparation time **15 minutes**
Cooking time **15 minutes**

2 tablespoons **butter**, plus extra for greasing
300 g (10 oz) **baby chestnut mushrooms**, sliced
6 **spring onions**, finely sliced
2 **garlic cloves**, crushed
500 g (1 lb) tub **fresh four-cheese sauce**
300 g (10 oz) **baby spinach leaves**
15 g (½ oz) **parsley**, finely chopped
2 tablespoons finely chopped **tarragon**
8 **ready-made savoury thin pancakes**
50 g (2 oz) **Parmesan-style vegetarian cheese**, grated
**salt** and **pepper**
**lettuce leaves**, to serve

**Heat** the butter in a large, nonstick frying pan, add the mushrooms, spring onions and garlic, and stir-fry over a high heat for 6–7 minutes.

**Stir** in half of the cheese sauce and heat until just bubbling. Add the spinach and cook for 1 minute until just wilted. Set aside, stir in the chopped herbs and season to taste.

**Take** 1 pancake and spoon one-eighth of the filling down the centre. Carefully roll the pancake up and put into a shallow, buttered gratin dish. Repeat with the remaining pancakes. Drizzle the remaining cheese sauce over the pancakes, scatter with the grated Parmesan and season to taste. Cook under a preheated medium-high grill for 3–4 minutes, until piping hot and turning golden.

**Remove** from the heat and serve with lettuce leaves.

**For creamy mushroom spaghetti**, cook 375 g (12 oz) quick-cook spaghetti according to the packet instructions. Meanwhile whizz 300 g (10 oz) chestnut mushrooms in a blender with 500 g (1 lb) tub ready-made fresh four-cheese sauce, then tip into a large saucepan and bring to the boil. Simmer for 2–3 minutes, then stir in 15 g (½ oz) chopped tarragon. Drain the pasta and add to the mushroom mixture, mix well, season and serve immediately.

# tarragon & cheddar cheese soufflé omelette

Serves **4**
Preparation time **10 minutes**
Cooking time **6–8 minutes**

**6 eggs**
15 g (½ oz) **tarragon,**
    chopped
100 g (3½ oz) **mature**
    **vegetarian Cheddar**
    **cheese**, grated
2 tablespoons **butter**
**crisp salad** and **crusty bread,**
    to serve

**Separate** the eggs and set aside the yolks. In a clean bowl, whisk the egg whites until stiff.

**Place** the egg yolks in a separate bowl with the tarragon and Cheddar cheese and lightly beat.

**Heat** the butter in a large heavy-based frying pan. Carefully fold the egg white mixture into the egg yolk mixture and add to the pan. Cook for 2–3 minutes over a high heat and then place under a preheated medium-hot grill for 3–4 minutes or until the top is souffléd and lightly golden.

**Serve** immediately with a crisp salad and crusty bread.

**For cheesy, tarragon and pasta gratin**, place 400 g (13 oz) cooked fusilli pasta in a lightly greased, shallow ovenproof dish. Whisk together 4 eggs, 15 g (½ oz) finely chopped tarragon, ¼ teaspoon cayenne pepper, 2 teaspoons Dijon mustard and 200 g (7 oz) grated vegetarian Cheddar cheese. Pour over the pasta, toss to mix well. Scatter over 100 g (3½ oz) grated Parmesan-style vegetarian cheese and bake in a preheated oven, 220°C (425°F), Gas Mark 7, for 15 minutes or until lightly golden on top. Serve immediately.

# flash-in-the-pan ratatouille

Serves **4**
Preparation time **15 minutes**
Cooking time **15 minutes**

100 ml (3½ fl oz) **olive oil**
2 **onions**, chopped
1 **aubergine**, cut into 1.5 cm
  (¾ in) cubes
2 large **courgettes**, cut into
  1.5 cm (¾ in) cubes
1 **red pepper**, deseeded and
  cut into 1.5 cm (¾ in) pieces
1 **yellow pepper**, deseeded
  and cut into 1.5 cm (¾ in)
  pieces
2 cloves **garlic**, crushed
1 × 400 g (13 oz) can
  **chopped tomatoes**
2–3 tablespoons **balsamic
  vinegar**
1 teaspoon **soft brown sugar**
10–12 **black olives**, pitted
**salt** and **pepper**
torn **basil leaves**, to garnish

**Heat** the oil in a large pan until very hot and stir-fry all
the vegetables and garlic, except the tomatoes, for a
few minutes.

**Add** the tomatoes, balsamic vinegar and sugar, season
with salt and pepper and stir well. Cover tightly and
simmer for 15 minutes until the vegetables are cooked.

**Remove** from the heat, scatter over the olives and torn
basil leaves and serve.

### For Mediterranean-style thick vegetable soup,

blend the cooked ratatouille from the above recipe with
300 ml (½ pint) hot vegetable stock until fairly smooth.
Ladle into warmed bowls and serve garnished with
basil leaves.

# spring onion, dill & chive pancakes

Serves **4**
Preparation time **15 minutes**
Cooking time **10–15 minutes**

175 g (6 oz) **plain flour**
1 teaspoon **baking powder**
150 ml (5 fl oz) **milk**
2 large **eggs**
50 g (2 oz) **butter**, melted
2 tablespoons each finely
   chopped **dill** and **chives**,
   plus extra to garnish
4 **spring onions**, finely
   chopped
**vegetable oil**, for shallow-
   frying
**salt** and **pepper**

**To serve**
200 g (7 oz) **soft cheese**,
   whisked with juice of
   1 **lemon**
2 **plum tomatoes**, finely
   chopped

**Sift** the flour and baking powder into a bowl with a pinch of salt. Whisk the milk, eggs, butter, herbs and spring onions together in a separate bowl.

**Stir** the wet mixture into the dry ingredients until the mixture comes together as a smooth, thick batter.

**Heat** a little vegetable oil in a small nonstick frying panand spoon in one-eighth of the batter. Cook the pancake for 1–2 minutes, or until bubbles form on the surface, then carefully turn it over and cook for a further 1–2 minutes, or until golden brown on both sides. Remove the pancake and keep warm while the remaining pancakes are cooked; the mixture makes 8 pancakes.

**Stack** 2 pancakes on each serving plate and spoon over a dollop of the cream cheese mixture. Top with the chopped tomatoes and serve garnished with a scattering of herbs and freshly ground black pepper.

**For scrambled eggs with dill, chives & cream cheese**, whisk together 6 eggs with 200 g (7 oz) soft cheese, then add a small handful each of chopped chives and dill. Heat 2 tablespoons butter in a large frying pan and add the egg mixture. Cook, stirring, until the eggs are scrambled. Season and serve over hot buttered toast.

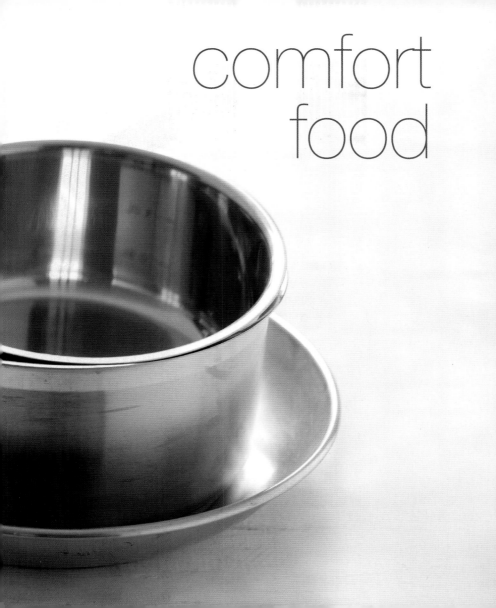

comfort
food

# quick roasted vegetable pizzas

Serves **4**
Preparation time **10 minutes**
Cooking time **12–15 minutes**

2 **ready-made chilled pizza
dough bases** (each about
23 cm/9 in in diameter)
400 g (13 oz) **ready-made
tomato pizza sauce**
16–20 **black olives**, pitted
400 g (13 oz) **roasted mixed
peppers in oil** (from a jar),
drained and roughly chopped
200 g (7 oz) **Sunblush
tomatoes**
3 tablespoons **caperberries**
8 **chargrilled artichoke
hearts in oil** (from a jar),
drained and quartered
250 g (8 oz) **vegetarian
mozzarella cheese**, diced
roughly chopped **parsley** or
**oregano leaves**, to garnish

**Preheat** the oven to 220°C (425°F), Gas Mark 7.

**Place** the pizza bases on 2 baking sheets.

**Spread** the pizza sauce evenly over the pizza bases
and scatter over the olives, roasted peppers, Sunblush
tomatoes, caperberries, artichoke hearts and mozzarella.

**Bake** in the preheated oven for 12–15 minutes until
golden and crispy.

**Remove** from the oven and garnish with the chopped
herbs before serving.

**For Mediterranean roasted pepper salad**, place
625 g (1 ¼ lb) roasted red and yellow peppers (from
a jar), drained, in a wide bowl with 25 pitted black
olives, 200 g (7 oz) Sunblush tomatoes, 25 g (1 oz)
caperberries, 8 quartered chargrilled artichoke hearts
and 250 g (8 oz) sliced vegetarian mozzarella cheese.
Toss in a handful of rocket leaves, drizzle with 50 ml
(2 fl oz) olive oil and the juice of 1 lemon. Season, toss
to mix well and serve.

# green vegetable curry

Serves **4**
Preparation time **15 minutes**
Cooking time **12–17 minutes**

1 tablespoon **sunflower oil**
3 tablespoons **vegetarian Thai green curry paste**
2 **red chillies**, deseeded and finely sliced (optional)
1 × 400 ml (14 fl oz) can **coconut milk**
200 ml (7 fl oz) **vegetable stock**
6 **dried lime leaves** or finely grated zest of 1½ **limes**
2 tablespoons **soy sauce**
1 tablespoon **soft brown sugar**
200 g (7 oz) **carrots**, cut into thick sticks
250 g (8 oz) **butternut squash**, peeled, deseeded and cut into 1.5 cm (¾ in) cubes
100 g (3½ oz) **sugarsnap peas**
25 g (1 oz) **coriander leaves**, very finely chopped
juice of **1 lime**
steamed **Thai fragrant jasmine rice**, to serve

**Heat** the oil in a large nonstick wok or saucepan. Add the curry paste and chillies, if using, and stir-fry for 2–3 minutes.

**Stir** in the coconut milk, stock, lime leaves or lime zest, soy sauce, sugar, carrots and butternut squash. Simmer, uncovered for 6–8 minutes, stirring occasionally.

**Add** the sugarsnaps and continue to simmer for 4–5 minutes.

**Remove** from the heat and stir in the coriander and lime juice.

**Serve** ladled into warmed bowls accompanied by steamed fragrant rice.

**For Thai green vegetable rice**, heat 1 tablespoon sunflower oil in a large wok or frying pan and add 2 sliced shallots and 200 g (7 oz) each of finely diced carrots, butternut squash and sliced sugarsnap peas. Stir-fry over a high heat for 4–5 minutes and then add 2 tablespoons vegetarian Thai green curry paste and 200 ml (7 fl oz) coconut milk. Stir and cook over a high heat for 4–5 minutes, then add 500 g (1 lb) cooked basmati rice. Stir and cook for 3 minutes or until well mixed and piping hot. Scatter over a small handful of chopped coriander, season and serve.

# mixed bean & tomato chilli

Serves **4**
Preparation time **10 minutes**
Cooking time **20–25 minutes**

2 tablespoons **olive oil**
1 **onion**, finely chopped
4 **garlic cloves**, crushed
1 teaspoon **red chilli flakes**
2 teaspoons **ground cumin**
1 teaspoon **cinnamon**
1 × 400 g (13 oz) can
  **chopped tomatoes**
1 × 400 g (13 oz) **can mixed**
  **beans**, rinsed and drained
1 × 400 g (13 oz) can **red**
  **kidney beans in chilli**
  **sauce**
**salt** and **pepper**

**To serve**
65 g (2½ oz) **soured cream**
25 g (1 oz) **coriander**, finely
  chopped
griddled **corn tortillas**

**Heat** the oil in a heavy-based saucepan and add the onion and garlic. Stir-fry for 3–4 minutes, then add the chilli, cumin and cinnamon.

**Stir-fry** for 2–3 minutes, then stir in the tomatoes. Bring the mixture to the boil, reduce the heat to medium and simmer gently for 10 minutes.

**Stir** in the beans and cook for 3–4 minutes until warmed through. Season well and served ladled into 4 warmed bowls.

**Top** each serving with a tablespoon of soured cream, garnish with chopped coriander and serve immediately with corn tortillas.

**For mixed bean, tomato & chilli bruschettas**, place ½ onion in a food processor with 2 crushed garlic cloves, 1 teaspoon red chilli flakes, 100 g (3½ oz) chopped tomatoes, 1 × 400 g (13 oz) can mixed beans, drained, and 15 g (½ oz) chopped flat leaf parsley. Whizz until fairly smooth, season and spread the mixture onto toasted ciabatta or sliced sourdough bread, drizzle with a little olive oil and serve.

# spinach dhal with cherry tomatoes

Serves **4**
Preparation time **15 minutes**
Cooking time **25–30 minutes**

300 g (10 oz) **red split lentils**
200 ml (7 fl oz) **coconut milk**
600 ml (1 pint) **vegetable stock**
1 teaspoon **ground cumin**
1 teaspoon **ground coriander**
1 teaspoon **turmeric**
1 teaspoon **ground ginger**
300 g (10 oz) **spinach,** chopped
200 g (7 oz) **cherry tomatoes**
¼ teaspoon **garam masala**
25 g (1 oz) **coriander** (leaves and stalks), finely chopped
**salt** and **pepper**
**naan bread** or **rice**, to serve

**Tarka**

2 tablespoons **sunflower oil**
4 **shallots**, thinly sliced
3 **garlic cloves**, thinly sliced
1 teaspoon finely chopped **fresh root ginger**
¼ teaspoon **chilli powder**
2 teaspoons **cumin seeds**
1 teaspoon **black mustard seeds**

**Place** the lentils in a sieve and rinse under cold running water until the water runs clear. Drain and transfer to a wide saucepan with the coconut milk, stock, cumin, coriander, turmeric and ginger. Bring the mixture to the boil, skimming off any scum as it rises to the surface, and cover. Reduce the heat and simmer for 15–20 minutes, stirring occasionally to prevent the mixture sticking to the bottom of the saucepan.

**Stir** in the spinach and cherry tomatoes and cook for 6–8 minutes, or until the lentils are soft and tender, adding a little stock or water if the mixture seems too thick.

**Meanwhile,** make the tarka. Heat the oil in a small frying pan and sauté the shallots, garlic, ginger, chilli powder, and cumin and mustard seeds, stirring often. Cook for 3–4 minutes until the shallots are lightly browned. Scrape this mixture into the cooked lentils.

**Stir** in the garam masala and chopped coriander, then check the seasoning. Serve with naan bread or rice.

**For curried lentil, tomato & spinach soup**, heat 2 × 400 g (13 oz) cans classic lentil soup in a large saucepan with 200 g (7 oz) baby spinach, 1 tablespoon mild curry powder and 200 g (7 oz) halved cherry tomatoes. Bring to the boil and simmer for 2–3 minutes until piping hot. Serve ladled into bowls and topped with a dollop of natural yogurt.

# romanesco cauliflower cheese

Serves **4**
Preparation time **10 minutes**
Cooking time **25–30 minutes**

8 baby **romanescos** or
  500 g (1 lb) large
  **cauliflower florets**
25 g (1 oz) **Parmesan-style
  vegetarian cheese**, grated

**Cheese sauce**
40 g (1½ oz) **butter**, plus extra
  for greasing
500 ml (17 fl oz) **full-fat milk**
40 g (1¼ oz) **plain flour**
2 **bay leaves**
a pinch of freshly grated
  **nutmeg**
300 g (10 oz) **vegetarian
  mature Cheddar**, grated
**salt** and **pepper**

**Trim** the base of each romanesco to flatten and lightly butter a shallow, ovenproof dish.

**Make** the sauce: melt the butter in a heavy-based saucepan. In a separate saucepan gently heat the milk. Stir the flour into the melted butter and cook over a low heat for 3 minutes, stirring. Remove the pan from the heat and pour in a little of the warmed milk, stirring continuously. Gradually add the rest of the milk, stirring continuously. Add the bay leaves and nutmeg and season well. Return the pan to a low heat and cook for 10–12 minutes, stirring frequently. Remove the bay leaves. Stir in the Cheddar and remove from the heat.

**Preheat** the grill to medium-high.

**Meanwhile,** cook the romanescos or cauliflower florets in boiling water for 5–6 minutes. Drain well, then place in the prepared dish, pour over the sauce and season.

**Scatter** over the Parmesan and cook under a preheated grill for 1 minute until lightly browned. Serve immediately.

**For creamy cauliflower soup**, place 500 g (1 lb) cauliflower florets, 1 chopped onion and 1 crushed garlic clove in a saucepan with 900 ml (1½ pints) hot vegetable stock. Bring to the boil, cover and cook over a medium heat for 12–15 minutes. Add 300 ml (½ pint) double cream and bring back to the boil. Remove from the heat and whizz using a hand-held blender until smooth. Season and stir in 200 g (7 oz) grated vegetarian Cheddar cheese just before serving.

# jewelled fruity spicy pilaf

Serves **4**

Preparation time **20 minutes**

Cooking time **12–15 minutes**, plus 10 minutes standing

400 g (13 oz) **basmati rice**

1 tablespoon **olive oil**

1 tablespoon **butter**

3 **shallots**, finely chopped

2 cloves **garlic**, finely chopped

4 **cardamom pods**, lightly bruised

2 **cloves**

2 **cinnamon sticks**

2 teaspoons **cumin seeds**

2 **carrots**, peeled and finely diced

1 litre (1¾ pints) hot **vegetable stock**

15 oz (½ oz) **dill**, chopped

300 g (10 oz) podded **edamame beans**

100 g (3½ oz) **sultanas**

100 g (3½ oz) **dried cranberries**

seeds from 1 ripe **pomegranate**

50 g (2 oz) **flaked pistachio nuts**

**salt** and **pepper**

**Rinse** the rice in cold running water and leave to drain.

**Heat** the oil and butter in a heavy-based saucepan and stir-fry the shallots and garlic for 1–2 minutes over a medium heat.

**Add** the cardamom pods, cloves, cinnamon sticks, cumin seeds, carrots and rice and stir to mix well. Add the stock along with the dill, season and bring to the boil. Stir in the edamame beans, sultanas and dried cranberries. Cover tightly and reduce the heat to low. Cook for 10–12 minutes without lifting the lid.

**Remove** from the heat and allow to stand, undisturbed, for 10 minutes.

**Take** the lid off (the liquid should have been completely absorbed), stir in the pomegranate seeds and pistachio nuts, season and serve immediately.

**For fruity spiced couscous**, place 400 g (13 oz) cooked couscous in a wide bowl with 1 finely julienned carrot, 2 finely sliced shallots, 100 g (3½ oz) sultanas, 100 g (3½ oz) chopped dill and 100 g (3½ oz) pomegranate seeds. Whisk together 75 ml (3 fl oz) olive oil with the juice of 1 orange, and 1 teaspoon each of ground cinnamon and cumin, then pour over the couscous mixture. Season, toss to mix well and serve.

# broccoli & mushrooms in black bean sauce with noodles

Serves **4**
Preparation time **15 minutes**
Cooking time **10–15 minutes**

1 tablespoon **sunflower oil**
1.5 cm (¾ in) piece of **ginger**, sliced into matchsticks
200 g (7 oz) **broccoli florets**
200 g (7 oz) **shiitake mushrooms**
6 **spring onions**, sliced into 1.5 cm (¾ in) lengths
1 **red pepper**, deseeded and sliced
300 ml (½ pint) **vegetable stock**
500 g (1 lb) **fresh egg noodles**
2 tablespoons **light soy sauce**
1 tablespoon **cornflour** mixed to a paste with 2 tablespoons water

**Black bean sauce**

1 tablespoon **fermented salted black beans**, rinsed
1 tablespoon **light soy sauce**
2 **garlic cloves**, crushed
1 **red chilli**, deseeded and chopped
1 tablespoon **Shaoxing rice wine**

**Place** all the ingredients for the black bean sauce in a food processor, blend until fairly smooth and set aside.

**Heat** a wok over high heat and add the oil. When smoking, add the ginger and stir-fry for a few seconds. Add the broccoli and stir-fry for a further 2–3 minutes.

**Add** the mushrooms, spring onions and red pepper and stir-fry for 2–3 minutes.

**Tip** in the black bean sauce and vegetable stock and bring to a simmer. Cook for 2–3 minutes until tender.

**Meanwhile,** cook the noodles according to the packet instructions, drain and keep warm.

**Add** the soy sauce, mix in the blended cornflour paste and cook to thicken for 1 minute. Serve immediately with the egg noodles.

### For broccoli, mushroom and black bean stir-fry,
heat 1 tablespoon vegetable oil in a large wok and add 300 g (10 oz) broccoli florets, 300 g (10 oz) sliced shiitake mushroom and 6 sliced spring onions. Stir-fry over a high heat for 3–4 minutes, then add a 125 g (4 oz) sachet of ready-made black bean stir-fry sauce and 100 ml (3½ fl oz) water. Stir-fry over a high heat for 3–4 minutes and serve over noodles.

# tagliatelle with pumpkin & sage

Serves **4**
Preparation time **10 minutes**
Cooking time **15–20 minutes**

875 g (1¾ lb) **pumpkin,
butternut** or **winter squash,**
peeled, deseeded and cut
into 1.5 cm (¾ in) cubes
50 ml (2 fl oz) **olive oil**
500 g (1 lb) fresh **tagliatelle**
50 g (2 oz) **rocket leaves**
8 **sage leaves**, chopped
grated **Parmesan-style
vegetarian cheese**, to serve
(optional)
**salt** and **pepper**

**Place** the pumpkin into a small roasting tin, drizzle over 2 tablespoons of the olive oil, season and toss to mix well. Roast in a preheated oven, 220°C (425°F), Gas Mark 7, for 15–20 minutes or until just tender.

**Meanwhile,** bring a large pan of salted water to the boil. Cook the pasta according to the packet instructions. Drain, return to the pan, then add the rocket, sage and pumpkin. Mix together over a gentle heat with the remaining olive oil until the rocket has wilted, then serve with a good grating of fresh Parmesan cheese, if desired.

**For roasted pumpkin tomato and sage soup**, place the roasted pumpkin from the above recipe into a saucepan with 600 ml (1 pint) hot vegetable stock, 200 ml (7 fl oz) passata and 1 tablespoon finely chopped sage leaves. Bring to the boil, then reduce the heat and simmer for 12–15 minutes. Using a hand-held blender, whizz the mixture until smooth. Stir in 100 ml (3½ fl oz) double cream and serve with warmed crusty bread.

# vegetable pad thai

Serves **4**
Preparation time **25 minutes**
Cooking time **12–15 minutes**

300 g (10½ oz) **flat rice noodles**
50 ml (2 fl oz) **vegetable oil**
500 g (1 lb) **firm tofu**, cut into 5 mm (¼ in) strips, patted dry
3 **garlic cloves**, finely chopped
2 **shallots**, finely chopped
300 g (10½ oz) **shiitake mushrooms**, torn or sliced
1–2 **red chillies**, deseeded and finely chopped
2 large **eggs**, beaten
bunch of **spring onions**, sliced
1 **carrot**, halved and finely sliced
handful of **chives**, snipped
bunch of **coriander**, chopped
100 g (3½ oz) **chilli roasted peanuts**
2 **limes**, cut into wedges

**Sweet and sour paste**
3 tablespoons **tamarind paste**
3 tablespoons **light soy sauce**
3 tablespoons **palm sugar**

**Place** the noodles in a large bowl and cover with warm water. Leave to soak for 10–15 minutes or until soft, then drain.

**Meanwhile,** make the sweet and sour paste. Mix the tamarind paste with a little hot water to loosen. Add the soy sauce and palm sugar, mix together and adjust to taste for a nice combination of sweet, salty and sour.

**Heat** 2 tablespoons of the oil in a wok or large frying pan. Fry the tofu for 3–4 minutes until golden and beginning to crisp. Remove from the wok, keep warm and set aside.

**Heat** the remaining oil in the wok and fry the garlic and shallots for 30 seconds. Add the mushrooms and red chillies and cook for 2 minutes until beginning to soften. Add the noodles and stir-fry for 2 minutes, then push to one side.

**Add** the eggs and allow them to set, then scramble and mix with the noodles. Tip in the sweet and sour paste and stir well. Toss in the onions, carrot and tofu and cook for a few minutes.

**Divide** among warmed serving bowls, scatter with the herbs and peanuts, and serve with the lime wedges.

# ravioli with sweet potato tomatoes & rocket

Serves **4**
Preparation time **15 minutes**
Cooking time **8–10 minutes**

50 g (2 oz) **butter**
375 g (12 oz) **sweet potato**,
  peeled and cut into 1 cm
  (½ in) cubes
2 **garlic cloves**, chopped
small handful of **sage leaves**,
  chopped
grated zest of ½ **lemon**, plus a
  squeeze of juice
200 g (7 oz) **cherry tomatoes**,
  halved
2 × 250 g (8 oz) packs **ready-
  made fresh cheese-filled
  ravioli**
**olive oil**, for drizzling
**salt** and **pepper**

**To serve**
100 g (3½ oz) **soft vegetarian
  goats' cheese**, crumbled
large handful of **rocket leaves**

**Melt** half the butter in a large frying pan, add the chopped sweet potato, season well, then fry over a medium heat for 5–6 minutes until golden brown all over.

**Add** the garlic, sage and lemon zest and fry for 1 minute.

**Add** the remaining butter, the tomatoes and lemon juice and gently fry over a low heat for 1 minute until melted.

**Meanwhile,** cook the ravioli according to the packet instructions. Drizzle with a little olive oil, then add the cooked pasta to the pan with the sweet potato and cherry tomatoes, and carefully stir to coat with the sauce.

**Spoon** into serving bowls and scatter with the goats' cheese, rocket leaves and black pepper before serving.

### For lemony sweet potato, ravioli and cherry tomato
**bake**, cook 2 × 250 g (8 oz) packs fresh ready-made cheese-filled ravioli according to the packet instructions, drain and add to a medium-sized, lightly greased baking dish along with 300 g (10 oz) halved cherry tomatoes and 200 g (7 oz) finely diced sweet potato. In a bowl, whisk together 3 eggs with 300 ml (½ pint) double cream, 2 tablespoons lemon zest, 1 crushed garlic clove, 2 teaspoons finely chopped sage leaves and 100 g (3½ oz) crumbled soft goats' cheese. Pour over the ravioli mixture and bake in a preheated oven, 200°C (400°F), Gas Mark 6, for 20 minutes or until golden and bubbling. Serve immediately with a rocket salad.

# deep-fried halloumi beer-batter fritters

Serves **4**
Preparation time **10 minutes**
Cooking time **15−20 minutes**

250 g (8 oz) **plain flour**
1 **egg**, separated
300 ml (½ pint) **ice-cold lager**
125 ml (4 fl oz) **ice-cold water**
**vegetable oil**, for deep-frying
500 g (1 lb) **vegetarian
 halloumi cheese**

**To serve**
**rocket leaves**
**lemon** wedges

**Sift** the flour into a large bowl and add the egg yolk. Gradually whisk in the lager, then add the measured water and whisk until well combined.

**Whisk** the egg white in a separate bowl until stiff peaks form. Fold this into the batter.

**Fill** a deep-fat fryer or a large, deep, heavy-based saucepan two-thirds full with vegetable oil. Heat the oil to 180°C (350°F) or until a cube of bread turns golden in 10−15 seconds.

**Cut** the halloumi into 1 cm (½ in) slices, then dip in the batter to coat. Fry the halloumi in batches for 3−4 minutes, or until crisp and golden-brown. Remove with a slotted spoon, season and serve on rocket leaves with wedges of lemon to squeeze over.

**For mixed pepper and halloumi skewers**, cut 2 red peppers, 2 yellow peppers, 2 red onions and 300 g (10 oz) halloumi cheese into bite-sized pieces. Place the vegetables and cheese in a wide bowl. Mix together 2 crushed garlic cloves, 125 ml (4 fl oz) olive oil, 2 teaspoons dried thyme and the juice and finely grated zest of 1 lemon. Pour over the cheese and vegetables and toss to mix. Thread the vegetables and cheese alternately onto 12 metal skewers. Season and grill under a preheated medium−high grill for 4−5 minutes on each side. Serve immediately.

# laksa-flavoured vegetable stew

Serves **4**
Preparation time **20 minutes**
Cooking time **25–30 minutes**

2 tablespoons **vegetable oil**
1 **onion**, thinly sliced
100 g (3½ oz) **vegetarian laksa curry paste**
2 × 400 ml (14 fl oz) cans **coconut milk**
300 ml (½ pint) **water**
1 teaspoon **salt**
200 g (7 oz) **potatoes**, peeled and cut into 1.5 cm (¾ in) cubes
250 g (8 oz) **carrots**, peeled and cut into 1.5 cm (¾ in) cubes
100 g (3½ oz) **fine green beans**, halved
150 g (5 oz) **cauliflower florets**
300 g (10 oz) **butternut squash**, peeled, deseeded and cut into 1.5 cm (¾ in) cubes
50 g (2 oz) **cashew nuts**
50 g (2 oz) **beansprouts**
4 **spring onions**, trimmed and sliced on the diagonal
handful of **Thai sweet basil** or **coriander leaves**

**Heat** the oil in a large pan over a medium heat. Add the onion and the curry paste and fry gently for 2–3 minutes until it begins to smell fragrant.

**Add** the coconut milk, measured water and salt and bring to the boil.

**Next,** add the potatoes and carrots and cook for 10 minutes, then add the green beans, cauliflower and squash and cook for a further 7 minutes.

**Add** the cashew nuts and simmer for 3 minutes until the vegetables are just tender.

**Stir** in the beansprouts, spring onions and basil or coriander. Simmer for 1 minute and serve immediately.

**For spicy coconut and vegetable noodles**, heat 1 tablespoon vegetable oil in a large wok or frying pan and add 6 sliced spring onions, 2 garlic cloves, 200 g (7 oz) each finely shredded carrots, mangetout and red pepper. Stir-fry for 4–5 minutes. Meanwhile, soak 375 g (12 oz) dried stir-fry rice noodles according to the packet instructions and then drain. Add 1 tablespoon vegetarian laksa curry paste to the frying pan and stir-fry for 3–4 minutes, then add 200 ml (7 fl oz) coconut cream along with the drained noodles. Stir-fry for 2–3 minutes, season and serve.

# pesto & antipasti puff tart

Serves **4**
Preparation time **10 minutes**
Cooking time **15–20 minutes**

375 g (12 oz) pack **ready-rolled puff pastry**
3 tablespoons **ready-made vegetarian pesto**
300 g (10 oz) **yellow** and **red cherry tomatoes**, halved
150 g (5 oz) **mixed antipasti** (artichokes, roasted peppers, mushrooms and aubergine), from a jar, drained
100 g (3½ oz) **vegetarian goats' cheese**, crumbled
**basil leaves**, to serve

**Lay** the puff pastry on a baking tray. Score a 2.5 cm (1 in) margin around the edge and prick the base with a fork.

**Top** with the pesto, cherry tomatoes, mixed antipasti and goats' cheese. Bake in a preheated oven, 200°C (400°F), Gas Mark 6, for 15–20 minutes.

**Top** with the basil leaves and serve.

**For antipasti and pesto pasta salad**, cook 300 g (10 oz) rigatoni or penne according to the packet instructions. Meanwhile, make the pesto by placing 50 g (2 oz) basil leaves, 25 g (1 oz) toasted pine nuts, 50 g (2 oz) grated Parmesan-style vegetarian cheese, 1 crushed garlic clove and 100 ml (3½ fl oz) olive oil in a blender and whizz until fairly smooth. Season with black pepper and place in a wide serving dish with 300 g (10 oz) halved cherry tomatoes and 200 g (7 oz) mixed antipasti (from a jar), then tip in the cooked pasta. Toss to mix well and serve at room temperature.

# spicy tofu & vegetable stir-fry

Serves **4**
Preparation time **15 minutes**
Cooking time **10 minutes**

50 ml (2 fl oz) **vegetable oil**
6 **spring onions**, finely sliced
2 **red chillies**, thinly sliced
2.5 cm (1 in) piece of **fresh
  root ginger**, finely chopped
4 **garlic cloves**, finely sliced
1 teaspoon crushed
  **Szechuan peppercorns**
pinch of **salt**
250 g (8 oz) **firm tofu**, cut into
  2.5 cm (1 in) cubes
200 g (7 oz) **mangetout**,
  halved
150 g (5 oz) **baby sweetcorn**,
  halved lengthways
250 g (8 oz) **pak choi**,
  chopped
300 g (10 oz) **beansprouts**
2 tablespoons **light soy sauce**
2 tablespoons **Shaoxing rice
  wine**
**sesame oil**, for drizzling
cooked **rice**, to serve

**Heat** 2 tablespoons of the vegetable oil in a wok or
deep frying pan and add the spring onions, chillies,
ginger, garlic, peppercorns and a pinch of salt. Fry for
1 minute, add the tofu and stir-fry for another 2 minutes,
then transfer to a plate.

**Heat** the remaining oil in the wok or pan and stir-fry the
mangetout, sweetcorn, pak choi and beansprouts for a
few minutes, until starting to wilt, then add the soy sauce
and rice wine.

**Return** the tofu mixture to the wok or pan and toss
everything together.

**Drizzle** with sesame oil and serve with cooked rice.

**For noodle and tofu salad with szechuan
peppercorns,** in a large bowl mix together 50 ml (2 fl oz)
light soy sauce, 3 tablespoons sweet chilli sauce, finely
grated zest and juice of 1 lemon, 2 chopped red chillies,
2 teaspoons Szechuan peppercorns and 2 tablespoons
water. Add 500 g (1 lb) firm tofu cubes and leave to
marinate for at least 25 minutes. Meanwhile, place
200 g (7 oz) fine rice noodles in a large bowl, cover with
boiling water and set aside for 5 minutes. Drain and cool
under running water. Toss together the cooled noodles,
100 g (3½ oz) thinly sliced mangetout, 100 g (3½ oz)
thinly sliced radishes, 1 thinly sliced red onion and
1 tablespoon toasted sesame seeds. Gently stir in the
tofu and marinade and divide among bowls. Scatter over
coriander leaves and serve.

# autumnal vegetable tagine

Serves **4**
Preparation time **10 minutes**
Cooking time **25 minutes**

2 tablespoons **olive oil**
1 **onion**, halved and thickly
  sliced
3 **garlic cloves**, finely chopped
1 teaspoon finely grated **fresh
  root ginger**
1 teaspoon **cinnamon**
pinch of **saffron threads**
2 teaspoons **ground cumin**
4 teaspoons **harissa paste**
65 g (2½ oz) **tomato purée**
3 tablespoons **clear honey**
875 g (1¾ lb) **mixed autumn
  vegetables,** such as squash,
  parsnips and sweet potato,
  peeled and cubed
750 ml (1¼ pints) **vegetable
  stock**
**salt** and **pepper**
**couscous**, to serve
chopped **coriander**, to garnish

**Heat** the oil in a large nonstick saucepan and sauté the onion and garlic for 1–2 minutes.

**Add** the ginger, cinnamon, saffron, ground cumin, harissa paste, tomato purée, honey, vegetables and stock and bring to the boil.

**Season** with salt and pepper, cover and simmer for 20 minutes or until the vegetables are very tender.

**Serve** with couscous and garnish with chopped coriander.

**For Moroccan-style couscous**, place 400 g (13 oz) couscous in a bowl with 2 teaspoons harissa paste, 1 teaspoon each of ground cumin and cinnamon, a large pinch of saffron, ½ chopped onion, 3 tablespoons tomato purée, 200 g (7 oz) chopped tomatoes and 1 tablespoon clear honey. Pour over hot vegetable stock to just cover. Season, stir, cover and allow to stand for 8 minutes or until all the liquid is absorbed. Fluff up with a fork, stir in 15 g (½ oz) chopped coriander and serve.

# aubergine & harissa sauté

Serves **4**
Preparation time **10 minutes**
Cooking time **7–10 minutes**

50 ml (2 fl oz) **sunflower oil**
750 g (1 ½ lb) baby
   **aubergines**, thinly sliced
4 **tomatoes**, chopped
1 teaspoon **ground cinnamon**
1 tablespoon finely chopped
   **coriander leaves**
2 tablespoons **harissa paste**
**salt** and **pepper**
cooked **basmati rice**, to serve

**Heat** the oil in a large frying pan and add the aubergines.

**Fry** over a high heat for 2–3 minutes, then add the tomatoes, cinnamon, coriander and harissa. Stir-fry for 3–4 minutes or until the aubergines are tender.

**Season** with salt and pepper to taste and serve with basmati rice.

### For crispy Moroccan-style aubergine and harissa fritters, cut 750 g (1 ½ lb) aubergines into thin sticks and mix in a bowl with 2 tablespoons harissa paste, 1 teaspoon turmeric, 1 teaspoon crushed coriander seeds and some salt. Add 250 g (8 oz) chickpea flour, a little at a time, stirring to coat the aubergine. Gradually drizzle cold water over the mixture, adding just enough to make a sticky batter. Fill a deep saucepan one-quarter full with sunflower oil and place over a high heat until it reaches 180°C (350°F) or a cube of bread it sizzles and turns golden in 10–15 seconds. Fry spoonfuls of the mixture in batches for 1–2 minutes or until golden brown and crisp on the outside. Remove with a slotted spoon and drain on kitchen paper. Serve with a minted yogurt dip.

# lemon & herb risotto

Serves **4**
Preparation time **15 minutes**
Cooking time **25–30 minutes**,
  plus 2–3 minutes standing

1 tablespoon **olive oil**
3 **shallots**, finely chopped
2 cloves **garlic**, finely chopped
½ head **celery**, finely chopped
1 **courgette**, finely diced
1 **carrot**, peeled and finely
  diced
300 g (10 oz) **arborio rice**
1.2 litres (2 pints) hot
  **vegetable stock**
good handful of **mixed herbs**
  (tarragon, parsley, chives,
  dill)
100 g (3½ oz) **butter**
1 tablespoon finely grated
  **lemon zest**
100 g (3½ oz) **Parmesan-
  style vegetarian cheese**,
  grated
**salt** and **pepper**

**Heat** the oil in a heavy-based saucepan, add the shallots, garlic, celery, courgette and carrot, and fry slowly for 4 minutes or until the vegetables have softened. Add the rice and turn up the heat. Stir-fry for 2–3 minutes.

**Add** a ladleful of hot stock followed by half the herbs and season well.

**Reduce** the heat to medium-low and add the remaining stock, 1 ladleful at at time, stirring constantly until each amount is absorbed and the rice is just firm to the bite but cooked through.

**Remove** from the heat and gently stir in the remaining herbs, butter, lemon zest and Parmesan. Place the lid on the pan and allow to sit for 2 to 3 minutes, during which time it will become creamy and oozy. Serve immediately, seasoned with freshly ground black pepper.

**For lemon & herb tagliatelle**, heat 1 tablespoon oil in a large frying pan and add 2 chopped shallots, 1 chopped garlic clove, ½ finely diced carrot and 1 finely diced celery stalk. Sauté over a medium heat for 4–5 minutes. Meanwhile cook 375 g (12 oz) tagliatelle according to the packet instructions. Drain and add to the frying pan with a large handful of chopped mixed herbs along with the juice and finely grated zest of 1 small lemon. Scatter over 100 g (3½ oz) grated Parmesan-style vegetarian and serve.

# asparagus & udon noodle stir-fry

Serves **4**
Preparation time **5 minutes**
Cooking time **5 minutes**

2 tablespoons **sunflower oil**
2 **garlic cloves**, crushed
400 g (13 oz) **asparagus tips**
8 **spring onions**, sliced
  diagonally
400 g (13 oz) **straight-to-wok
  udon noodles**
75 ml (3 fl oz) **oyster sauce**
75 ml (3 fl oz) **water**

**Heat** the oil in a large frying pan. Add the garlic and asparagus tips and stir-fry for 2 minutes.

**Add** the spring onions, noodles, oyster sauce and water and toss together. Stir-fry for a further 2 minutes, then serve immediately.

**For udon noodle pancakes with griddled asparagus**, cook 200 g (7 oz) udon noodles according to the packet instructions. Drain and set aside. Heat 2 tablespoons vegetable oil in a frying pan over a high heat. Divide the noodles into 12 portions and fry in batches. Flatten with a spatula, so the surface browns, reduce the heat to medium-high and cook the noodle 'pancakes' for 3–4 minutes or until golden and crispy on the base. Turn and cook for 1–2 minutes more, again flattening them as they cook. Remove and keep warm. Heat a griddle pan until smoking. Brush 400 g (13 oz) asparagus tips with oil and sear for 2–3 minutes on each side. Transfer to a bowl and mix with 100 ml (3½ fl oz) oyster sauce and 3 tablespoons sweet chilli sauce. Serve the noodle 'pancakes' immediately topped with the asparagus mixture.

# tomato, camembert, goats' cheese & herb tart

Serves **4**
Preparation time **20 minutes**
Cooking time **15–18 minutes**

250 g (8 oz) **puff pastry**
50 g (2 oz) **black olive**
   tapenade or **Dijon mustard**,
   if preferred
300 g (10 oz) **ripe plum**
   **tomatoes**, finely sliced
8 large **basil leaves**, roughly
   torn
125 g (4 oz) **vegetarian**
   **Camembert cheese**
100 g (3½ oz) **vegetarian**
   **goats' cheese**
2 tablespoons **thyme leaves**,
   plus extra to garnish
1–2 tablespoons **extra virgin**
   **olive oil**
**salt** and **pepper**

**Roll** out the pastry and use it to line a 25 cm (10 in) tart tin.

**Spread** the tapenade or mustard over the base of the tart.

**Discarding** any juice or seeds that have run from the tomatoes, lay the slices in concentric circles in the tart. Season the tomatoes (bear in mind that tapenade is salty) and scatter over the basil.

**Cut** the Camembert into thin wedges and the goats' cheese into thin wedges or slices, according to its shape. Arrange a circle of Camembert pieces around the outside and a circle of goats' cheese within. Put any remaining pieces of cheese in the middle.

**Scatter** over the thyme leaves and drizzle the oil on top.

**Bake** in a preheated oven, 200°C (400°F), Gas Mark 6, for 15–18 minutes until the pastry is cooked and the cheese is golden and bubbling. Serve immediately, garnished with thyme.

**For tomato, tapenade & two cheese baguette**, split 2 warmed baguettes and spread both sides with 150 g (5 oz) black olive tapenade and 100 g (3½ oz) Dijon mustard. Fill each with 400 g (13 oz) ripe, sliced plum tomatoes, 25 g (1 oz) basil leaves, 100 g (3½ oz) each of sliced vegetarian Camembert cheese and vegetarian goats' cheese. Season and serve with a green salad.

# butter bean & vegetable nut crumble

Serves **4**
Preparation time **10 minutes**
Cooking time **20–25 minutes**

2 × 250 g (8 oz) packs
  **prepared broccoli,
  cauliflower** and **carrots**
500 g (1 lb) jar **ready-made
  tomato and herb sauce**
2 **garlic cloves**, crushed
20 g (¾ oz) **basil leaves**,
  finely chopped
1 × 400 g (13 oz) can **butter
  beans**, drained and rinsed

**Crumble topping**
75 g (3 oz) **butter**, chilled and
  diced
175 g (6 oz) **plain flour**
100 g (3½ oz) **walnuts**,
  chopped
50 g (2 oz) **vegetarian
  Cheddar cheese**, grated
**salt** and **pepper**

**For** the crumble topping, rub the butter into the plain flour until crumbs form. Stir in the chopped walnuts and grated cheese, season and set aside.

**Remove** the carrots from the packs of prepared vegetables, roughly chop and boil for 2 minutes. Add the broccoli and cauliflower and cook for another minute, then drain.

**Meanwhile,** heat the tomato and herb sauce in a large saucepan until bubbling.

**Stir** in the garlic, basil, butter beans and blanched vegetables. Transfer to a medium-sized ovenproof dish and scatter over the crumble mixture. Bake in a preheated oven, 200°C (400°F), Gas Mark 6, for 15–20 minutes or until golden and bubbling.

**For vegetable & butter bean soup**, lightly fry 2 sliced cloves garlic and 1 chopped onion in 2 tablespoons olive oil for 1–2 minutes. Add 1 litre (1¾ pints) hot vegetable stock, 2 × 250 g (8 oz) packs prepared broccoli, cauliflower and carrots, 25 g (1 oz) chopped parsley and 2 × 400 g (13 oz) cans butter beans, drained, to the onion, and simmer for 15 minutes. Allow the soup to cool slightly, then blend two-thirds using a hand-held blender. Return the blended soup to the vegetables along with 2 tablespoons tomato purée and mix well. Serve immediately, garnished with chopped parsley, if desired.

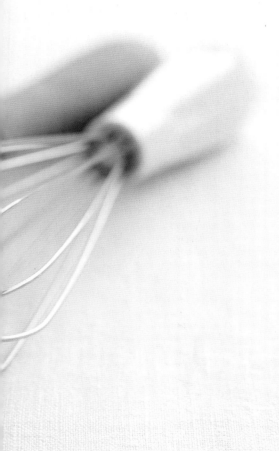

# desserts

# cookie dough brownies

Makes 12–16
Preparation time **15 minutes**
Cooking time **18–20 minutes**

150 g (5 oz) **unsalted butter**,
  plus extra for greasing
150 g (5 oz) **plain dark
  chocolate**, broken into small
  pieces
2 large **eggs**
125 g (4 oz) **caster sugar**
50 g (2 oz) **self-raising flour**
pinch of **salt**
200 g (7 oz) **shop-bought
  chilled cookie dough**,
  chopped
50 ml (2 fl oz) **sweetened
  condensed milk**

**Grease** a 30 × 20 cm (12 × 8 in) brownie tin and
line with nonstick baking paper. Place the butter and
chocolate in a small saucepan over a low heat and
warm until just melted.

**Meanwhile,** place the eggs and sugar in a large bowl
and whisk until combined. Using a rubber spatula, stir in
the melted chocolate, flour, salt and cookie dough.

**Scrape** the mixture into the prepared tin and drizzle
over the condensed milk.

**Bake** in a preheated oven, 200°C (400°F), Gas Mark 6,
for 15–18 minutes until just firm to the touch, but with a
slightly fudgy texture.

**Leave** to cool in the tin for 1–2 minutes, then lift on
to a board using the lining paper and cut into 12–16
squares. Serve warm or cold.

**For cookie dough brownie pudding**, arrange
4 halved shop-bought chocolate brownies in a
medium-sized, ovenproof dish and scatter over 50 g
(2 oz) chopped walnuts, 50 g (2 oz) baking fudge
chunks and 100 g (3½ oz) shop-bought chilled cookie
dough, chopped. Pour over 300 g (10 oz) shop-bought
Belgian chocolate sauce. Bake in a preheated oven,
200°C (400°F), Gas Mark 6, for 10–12 minutes until
bubbling. Serve with ice cream.

# mixed berry eton mess

Serves **4**

Preparation time **10 minutes**

400 g (13 oz) **mixed berries**
(such as blackberries,
raspberries, blueberries),
plus extra to decorate
400 ml (14 fl oz) **strawberry
yogurt**
300 ml (½ pint) **crème fraîche**
25 g (1 oz) **icing sugar**
4 **meringue nests**, roughly
crushed

**Place** half the berries in a blender and blend until smooth. Transfer to a bowl with the strawberry yogurt and stir to mix well.

**Place** the remaining berries in a bowl and mix in the crème fraîche and icing sugar. Add this mixture to the berry and yogurt mixture and swirl through to create a marbled effect.

**Fold** in the crushed meringue and spoon into 4 chilled dessert glasses.

**Serve** immediately, decorated with berries.

**For summer berry trifles**, gently cook 200 g (7 oz) each raspberries, blueberries and blackberries, 50 g (2 oz) caster sugar and 2 tablespoons water in a small pan for 2–3 minutes until the fruit is just soft. Allow to cool. Break 4 trifle sponges into small pieces and use to line 4 individual dessert bowls or glasses. Spoon over the berry mixture followed by 200 ml (7 fl oz) fresh vanilla custard. Top each with a spoonful of crème fraîche and chill until ready to serve.

# quick mini lemon meringue pies

Serves **4**
Preparation time **10 minutes**
Cooking time **5–6 minutes**

4 individual **sweet pastry
 cases**
175 g (6 oz) **lemon curd**
1 **egg white**
50 g (2 oz) **caster sugar**

**Fill** each pastry case with one-quarter of the lemon curd.

**In** a large, clean bowl, whisk the egg white until it forms soft peaks and hold its shape. Gradually whisk in the sugar, a little at a time, until the mixture is thick and glossy.

**Pipe** the meringue mixture in swirls over the lemon curd and bake on the top shelf of a preheated oven, 200°C (400°F), Gas Mark 6, for 5–6 minutes or until the meringue is just beginning to brown. Cool slightly and serve.

**For lemon meringue & blueberry pots**, roughly crush 2 meringue nests and place in the base of 4 dessert bowls. Whip 200 ml (7 fl oz) double cream until softly peaked and then stir in 125 g (4 oz) lemon curd to create a marbled effect. Spoon this mixture over the crushed meringue and top each with 25 g (1 oz) blueberries.

# berry, honey & yogurt pots

Serves **4**
Preparation time **15 minutes**

400 g (13 oz) **frozen mixed
  berries**, thawed
juice of 1 **orange**
75 ml (3 fl oz) **clear honey**
400 ml (14 fl oz) **vanilla
  yogurt**
50 g (2 oz) **granola**

**Whizz** half the berries with the orange juice and honey in a blender until fairly smooth.

**Transfer** to a bowl and stir in the remaining berries.

**Divide** one-third of the berry mixture among 4 dessert glasses or small bowls. Top with half the yogurt.

**Layer** with half the remaining berry mixture and top with the remaining yogurt.

**Top** with the remaining berry mixture and scatter over the granola just before serving.

**For berry & yogurt filo tartlets**, cut 2 large sheets of filo pastry in half and cut each half into 4 squares. Brush each square with melted butter. Stack 4 squares on top of each other and repeat with the remaining squares to create 4 stacks. Use to line four 10 cm (4 in) diameter deep tartlet tins. Bake the filo cases for 8–10 minutes in a preheated oven, 180°C (350°F), Gas Mark 4, until crispy and golden. Allow to cool and remove from the tins. To serve, place 2 tablespoons vanilla yogurt into each tartlet case and spoon over 200 g (7 oz) mixed berries. Dust with icing sugar and serve immediately.

# mango & custard fools

Serves **4**
Preparation time **15 minutes**

4 firm, ripe, **sweet mangoes**
200 ml (7 fl oz) canned
   **mango purée**
50 g (2 oz) **caster sugar**
150 ml (¼ pint) **double cream**
¼ teaspoon crushed
   **cardamom seeds**, plus extra
   to decorate
200 ml (7 fl oz) **ready-made
   fresh custard**

**Peel** and stone the mango and cut the flesh into small bite-sized cubes. Place three-quarters of the mango in a blender along with the mango purée and sugar and blend until smooth.

**Lightly** whisk the cream with the cardamom seeds until softly peaked, then gently fold in the custard. Lightly fold one-quarter of the mango mixture into the custard mixture to give a marbled effect.

**Divide** half the remaining mango cubes among 4 individual serving glasses and top with half the fool. Layer over half the remaining mango mixture.

**Decorate** with the remaining mango cubes and a scattering of crushed cardamom seeds and chill until ready to serve.

**For mango & cardamom lassi**, peel and stone 3 ripe mangoes and place the flesh in a blender with 75 g (3 oz) of clear honey, 500 ml (17 fl oz) natural yogurt and 1 teaspoon crushed cardamom seeds. Whizz until smooth, pour into 4 tall, ice-filled glasses and serve.

# spiced drop scones with ice cream & chocolate sauce

Serves **4**
Preparation time **10 minutes**
Cooking time **10–15 minutes**

250 g (8 oz) **self-raising flour**
1 teaspoon **ground cinnamon**
1 teaspoon **allspice**
50 g (2 oz) **caster sugar**
1 **egg**
300 ml (½ pint) **milk**
**sunflower oil**, for shallow-
  frying

**To serve**
4 scoops **vanilla ice cream**
125 g (4 oz) **ready-made
  chocolate sauce**

**Place** the flour, cinnamon, allspice and sugar in bowl and make a well in the centre.

**Beat** the egg and pour it into the centre of the flour mixture.

**Gradually** add the milk, beating well until smooth.

**Heat** a little oil in a heavy-based frying pan or griddle until moderately hot.

**Working** in batches, drop large tablespoons of the mixture into the pan and cook for 1–2 minutes until bubbles appear on the surface and the underneath is golden brown. Turn the drop scone over and cook the other side for 1–2 minutes. Place a tea towel or kitchen paper between each scone and keep warm on a plate in a preheated oven, 150°C (300°F), Gas Mark 2. Repeat until all the batter has been used.

**Serve** 3 drop scones per person with scoops of vanilla ice cream and drizzle over the chocolate sauce.

# blueberry pancakes

Serves **4**
Preparation time **10 minutes**
Cooking time **10–15 minutes**

250 ml (8 fl oz) **milk**
2 **eggs**
100 g (3½ oz) **caster sugar**
75 g (3 oz) **butter**, melted,
  plus extra for greasing
1 teaspoon **baking powder**
pinch of **salt**
250 g (8 oz) **plain flour**
100 g (3½ oz) **blueberries**,
  plus extra to serve
**maple syrup** or **clear honey**,
  to serve

**Whisk** together the milk, eggs, sugar and melted butter in a large bowl. Whisk in the baking powder and salt, add half the flour and whisk well until all the ingredients are incorporated, then whisk in the remaining flour. Stir in the blueberries to mix well.

**Heat** a large, nonstick pan over a medium-high heat. Grease the base of the pan with a little melted butter using kitchen paper. Lower the heat to medium. Spoon in large tablespoons of the batter until the pan is full, allowing a little space between each pancake. Add extra butter for frying if required.

**Cook** for 1–2 minutes on each side or until golden brown, then keep warm on a plate in a preheated oven, 150°C (300°F), Gas Mark 2. Repeat until all the batter has been used.

**Divide** the pancakes among 4 warmed plates and drizzle over a little maple syrup or honey. Serve immediately with extra blueberries.

**For blueberry cheesecake pots**, crush 4 ginger biscuits and place in the base of 4 individual dessert glasses. Mix together 250 g (8 oz) mascarpone, 50 ml (2 fl oz) double cream, 25 g (1 oz) icing sugar and the juice and grated zest of 1 lemon. Spoon over the biscuit base, top with 150 g (5 oz) blueberries and serve.

# french toast with blueberries & redcurrants

Serves **4**
Preparation time **10 minutes**
Cooking time **12–15 minutes**

3 **eggs**
100 ml (3½ fl oz) **milk**
50 ml (2 fl oz) **double cream**
100 g (3½ oz) **caster sugar**
2 teaspoons **ground cinnamon**
6 thick slices **white bread**
400 g (13 oz) **mixed blueberries** and **redcurrants**
2 tablespoons **water**
75 g (3 oz) **butter**
**crème fraîche**, to serve

**Whisk** together the eggs, milk, cream, half the sugar and a pinch of the cinnamon in a large bowl.

**Soak** the bread in the egg mixture for a couple of minutes.

**In** a pan, mix the remaining cinnamon with the remaining caster sugar, then toss the berries in the mixture until they are well coated. Add the water and heat the mixture over a medium heat for 3–4 minutes. Remove from the heat and keep warm.

**Melt** half the butter in a separate large nonstick frying pan. Drain 3 slices of bread and fry for 2–3 minutes on each side or until golden brown. Repeat with the remaining butter and bread. Drain the toast on kitchen paper, cut each in half diagonally, and arrange the slices on serving plates that have been warmed in a preheated oven, 150°C (300°F), Gas Mark 2.

**Spoon** the berry mixture around and serve immediately with a dollop of crème fraîche.

**For crunchy creamy berry sundaes**, whisk 400 ml (14 fl oz) double cream in a bowl. Roughly break 2 meringue nests into the cream and add 100 g (3½ oz) redcurrants and 200 g (7 oz) blueberries. Gently fold together so that the fruit is marbled through the cream. Place a large scoop of vanilla ice cream in the bottom of 4 sundae glasses and top with spoonfuls of the berry cream and dust with icing sugar.

# instant summer berry sorbet

Serves **4**
Preparation time **5 minutes**

300 g (10 oz) **frozen summer
  berries**
400 ml (14 fl oz) **raspberry
  yogurt**
50 g (2 oz) **icing sugar**

**Tip** the frozen berries, yogurt and sugar into a food
processor or blender. Whizz until blended.

**Scrape** the mixture from the sides and blend again.

**Spoon** into chilled glasses or bowls and serve
immediately.

**For frozen berries with white & dark hot
chocolate sauce**, divide 400 g (13 oz) frozen mixed
berries among 4 chilled serving plates or shallow
bowls. Melt 100 g (3½ oz) dark chocolate and
100 g (3½ oz) white chocolate in 2 separate small
pans. Whisk 150 ml (¼ pint) double cream until
softly peaked. When ready to serve, drizzle the hot
chocolate sauces over the frozen berries and serve
immediately with a dollop of the whipped cream.

# peach & raspberry mascarpone pots

Serves **4**
Preparation time **15 minutes**

150 g (5 oz) **mascarpone
 cheese**
finely grated zest and juice of
 1 **lemon**
75 g (3 oz) **caster sugar**, plus
 1 tablespoon
150 ml (5 fl oz) **double cream**
400 g (13 oz) **raspberries**
4 **ripe peaches**

**Beat** the mascarpone with the lemon zest and juice and sugar until smooth.

**Whisk** the cream until it just holds its shape then fold into the cheese mixture.

**Pulse** one-quarter of the raspberries in a food processor or blender with the remaining 1 tablespoon caster sugar for 1–2 minutes or until smooth. Transfer to a bowl. Fold in the remaining berries.

**Peel,** stone and cut the peaches into thick slices and arrange half the slices in the base of 4 dessert glasses or bowls.

**Spoon** half the cheese mixture over the peaches and then top with the raspberry mixture. Continue to layer, finishing off with the raspberry mixture. Chill until ready to serve.

**For peach & raspberry salad with lemon mascarpone**, arrange slices of peaches from 4 ripe, peeled and stoned peaches on a serving platter with 200g (7 oz) raspberries. Whisk together 100 g (3½ oz) mascarpone with 75 ml (3 fl oz) double cream, the juice and finely grated zest of ½ lemon and 50 g (2 oz) caster sugar. Serve the fruit salad with a generous dollop of the cream mixture.

# chocolate fondue

Serves **4**
Preparation time **5 minutes**
Cooking time **5 minutes**

400 g (13 oz) **dark chocolate**,
  broken into small pieces
25 g (1 oz) **unsalted butter**
150 ml (¼ pint) **double cream**
50 ml (2 fl oz) **milk**
**strawberries** and
  **marshmallows**, for dipping

**In** a small saucepan, gently heat the chocolate, butter, cream and milk, stirring occasionally, until the chocolate is melted and the sauce is glossy and smooth. Transfer to a warmed bowl or fondue pot.

**Thread** 1 or 2 strawberries and marshmallows onto skewers, dip into the dark chocolate fondue and eat immediately.

**For chocolate-stuffed croissants with strawberries**, line a baking sheet with baking paper. Chop a 200 g (7 oz) bar of dark chocolate into small squares. Split open 4 croissants and tuck the chocolate squares inside each one. Place the croissants on the baking sheet and bake in a preheated oven, 160°C (325°F), Gas Mark 3, for 8–10 minutes or until the chocolate melts and the croissants are warmed through. Dust the croissants with icing sugar and serve with scoops of vanilla ice cream and strawberries.

# spiced caramelized pineapple with rum

Serves **4**
Preparation time **10 minutes**
Cooking time **8–10 minutes**

50 g (2 oz) **butter**
50 g (2 oz) **caster sugar**
1 **pineapple**, peeled and
   cored, or 625 g (1¼ lb)
   **canned pineapple**, the flesh
   cut into bite-sized pieces
2–3 **star anise**
1 **cinnamon stick**
2–3 tablespoons of **dark
   rum cream** or **ice cream**,
   to serve

**Heat** the butter in a large frying pan until it begins to foam.

**Add** the sugar, pineapple, star anise and cinnamon stick and cook for 5–6 minutes over a high heat, stirring continuously, until the sugar mixture starts to caramelize.

**Pour** in the rum and stir to mix well. Cook for a further 1–2 minutes, then remove from the heat and serve immediately with a dollop of cream or ice cream.

**For pineapple skewers with spiced sugar**, using a pestle and mortar grind together 50 g (2 oz) caster sugar, 1 teaspoon ground cinnamon and 1 teaspoon crushed star anise. Thread 500 g (1 lb) pineapple cubes onto 8 wooden skewers. Scatter with the spiced sugar and serve with a dollop of cream.

# fresh berry tart

Serves **4**
Preparation time **15 minutes**
Cooking time **12–15 minutes**

**plain flour**, for rolling out the
pastry
1 × 375 g (12 oz) **block puff
pastry**
200 ml (7 fl oz) **double cream**
75 ml (3 fl oz) **ready-made
fresh vanilla custard**
1 tablespoon **kirsch** or **cherry
liqueur**
300 g (10 oz) **blackberries**
200 g (7 oz) **raspberries**
200 g (7 oz) **blueberries**
**icing sugar**, to dust

**On** a surface dusted with flour, thinly roll out the pastry
to fit a 23 cm (9 in) diameter tart tin. Trim the edges
with a sharp knife and place on a baking sheet.

**Using** the tip of a knife, score the pastry 1.5 cm (¾ in)
from the edge to form a border.

**Bake** the pastry case in a preheated oven, 220°C (425°F),
Gas Mark 7, for 12–15 minutes or until puffed up and golden.

**Remove** from the oven and press the base of the
pastry down to create a shell with raised sides. Set
aside to cool.

**Whisk** the cream until stiff, then mix in the custard and
kirsch or liqueur. Spoon into the centre of the cooled
pastry base.

**Arrange** the fruit attractively on the cream mixture, dust
with icing sugar and serve immediately.

**For berry & lemon syllabubs**, crumble 4 shortbread
biscuits into the bottom of 4 sundae glasses. Drizzle
1 tablespoon kirsch into each glass. Whisk 250 ml (8 fl oz)
double cream in a bowl and add 25 g (1 oz) icing sugar.
Add 125 g (4 oz) lemon curd and 200 g (7 oz) lightly
crushed mixed berries and lightly fold to create a marbled
effect. Spoon the cream mixture into the glasses. Top
with 2 tablespoons flaked almonds and a sprig of mint
and serve.

# rhubarb, orange & stem ginger pots

Serves **4**
Preparation time **15 minutes**
Cooking time **5 minutes**

300 g (10 oz) **rhubarb**
2 pieces of **stem ginger in syrup** (from a jar), drained and finely chopped
50 g (2 oz) **caster sugar**
2 **cloves**
1 **cinnamon stick**
2 **oranges**, 1 juiced and 1 peeled and segmented
50 g (2 oz) **mascarpone cheese**
100 ml (3½ fl oz) **natural yogurt**

**Cut** the rhubarb into bite-sized pieces and place in a saucepan with half the ginger, the sugar, cloves, cinnamon stick and orange juice.

**Place** over a high heat and when bubbling, reduce the heat, cover with a lid and simmer, stirring occasionally, for 4–5 minutes or until just tender. Discard the cloves and cinnamon and allow to cool.

**Divide** the orange segments among 4 dessert glasses. Whisk together the mascarpone and yogurt until smooth, then layer alternately with the rhubarb and the mascarpone mixture in the glasses.

**Chill** until ready to serve, topping each with the remaining chopped ginger.

**For rhubarb & stem ginger crumbles**, grease four 300 ml (½ pint) ramekins or ovenproof dishes. Place 400 g (13 oz) rhubarb chopped into 2.5 cm (1 in) pieces into the ramekins. Add 2 tablespoons finely chopped stem ginger with a little of the syrup from the jar and scatter over 1 teaspoon caster sugar. Divide 200 ml (7 fl oz) fresh ready-made custard among the ramekins and set aside. Rub together 100 g (3½ oz) plain flour with 75 g (3 oz) butter until it resembles breadcrumbs. Stir in 50 g (2 oz) caster sugar and scatter over the custard. Bake in a preheated oven, 180°C (350°F), Gas Mark 4, for 15 minutes, or until bubbling and golden.

# luscious victoria & strawberry sponge

Serves **4**
Preparation time **10 minutes**

1 **ready-made round sponge cake** (about 15 cm/6 in diameter)
150 g (5 oz) **double cream**
200 g (7 oz) **small strawberries**, halved
150 g (5 oz) **good-quality strawberry jam**
**icing sugar**, to dust

**Halve** the sponge cake horizontally and place the base on a serving plate.

**Whip** the cream until softly peaked and spread it over the cut side of the base.

**Mix** together the strawberries and jam and spoon carefully over the cream.

**Top** with the sponge lid, press down lightly and dust the top with icing sugar. Cut into thick slices and serve immediately.

**For strawberry shrikhand**, hull and roughly chop 300 g (10 oz) strawberries and place in a bowl with 2 tablespoons rosewater and 50 g (2 oz) icing sugar. Line 4 dessert bowls with a thick slice of sponge cake and spoon over the strawberry mixture. Whisk together 400 g (13 oz) thick Greek yogurt with 150 g (5 oz) strawberry jam and spoon over the strawberry mixture. Chill until ready to serve.

# tropical fruit trifles

Serves **4**
Preparation time **15 minutes**

1 large **passionfruit**
2 tablespoons **icing sugar** (to taste)
juice of 1 **orange**
4 **kiwi fruits**
1 **mango**
10–12 **seedless green** and **red grapes**
4 thick slices **sponge cake**
400 ml (14 fl oz) **ready-made fresh custard**

**Topping**
100 ml (3½ fl oz) **double cream**, softly whipped
julienned **orange zest**, to decorate

**Prepare** the fruit by scraping the seeds from a passionfruit into a large mixing bowl. Mix in the icing sugar and orange juice.

**Peel** and finely dice the kiwi fruits. Stone and peel the mango, then cut the flesh into 1 cm (½ in) dice.

**Add** the diced fruit to the passionfruit mixture with the grapes. Chill until ready to serve.

**To** assemble the trifles, take 4 dessert bowls or glasses and arrange the cake and fruit salad in the base. Pour the custard over the top.

**Place** a dollop of whipped cream on top of the custard and serve decorated with the orange zest.

**For tropical fruit salad**, place 1 cubed mango in a bowl with 300 g (10 oz) cubed pineapple, 4 peeled and cubed kiwi fruit and 200 g (7 oz) seedless green and red grapes. Add the juice of 1 orange and 50 g (2 oz) icing sugar and toss to mix well. Serve with ice cream.

# watermelon, lime & grenadine squares

Serves **4**
Preparation time **10 minutes**
Cooking time **8–10 minutes**

50 ml (2 fl oz) **grenadine**
50 g (2 oz) **caster sugar**
finely grated zest and juice of
   1 **lime**, plus extra **lime zest**
   to decorate
100 ml (3½ fl oz) **water**
1 small–medium **watermelon**

**Place** the grenadine, sugar and lime juice and zest with the measured water in a small saucepan and bring to the boil. Reduce the heat and cook gently for 6–8 minutes until thick and syrupy. Remove from the heat and allow to cool.

**Meanwhile**, halve the watermelon and, using a sharp knife, slice the rind from the bottom of each half.

**Lay** the halves on a chopping board and, working from top to bottom, trim the rind from the watermelon flesh in 4 cuts, creating 2 large squares.

**Cut** each square of watermelon into equal bite-sized squares and place on a serving platter to form a neat large square (made up of the bite-sized squares).

**Drizzle** over the cooled grenadine syrup, scatter over the lime zest and serve immediately.

### For iced watermelon lime & grenadine coolers,
whizz the flesh of ½ a watermelon in a blender with 50 ml (2 fl oz) grenadine, 50 g (2 oz) caster sugar, 15 g (½ oz) chopped mint leaves and the juice and finely grated zest of 1 lime. Fill 4 tall glasses with crushed ice, pour over the watermelon mixture and serve immediately.

# blackberry & apple cranachan

Serves **4**

Preparation time **10 minutes**

Cooking time **5–10 minutes**

4 teaspoons **porridge oats**

8 teaspoons **caster sugar**

250 g (8 oz) **vanilla yogurt**

½ teaspoon **ground cinnamon**

1 tablespoon **whisky** (optional)

400 g (13 oz) **blackberries**, plus extra for decoration

2 tablespoons **butter**

1 **dessert apple**, peeled, cored and coarsely grated

**Place** a small frying pan over a medium high heat. Add the oats and cook for 1 minute, then add 3 teaspoons of the sugar. Dry-fry, stirring for 2–3 minutes, or until the oats are lightly browned, then tip onto a piece of nonstick baking paper and leave to cool.

**Mix** together the yogurt, cinnamon, 1 teaspoon of the sugar and the whisky, if using.

**Stir** in the blackberries, crushing them slightly.

**Heat** a nonstick pan over a high heat, add the butter and sauté the apple for 3–4 minutes. When the apple begins to soften, add the remaining sugar and cook until lightly browned. Set aside to cool.

**Layer** the blackberry mix with the apple mix in 4 dessert glasses. Top with the oat mix and blackberries, then serve.

### For individual crunchy blackberry & apple crumbles,
peel and chop 625 g (1 ¼ lb) Bramley apples into small chunks. Squeeze the juice of ½ lemon over the apple and mix well. In four 300 ml (½ pint) ramekins, layer the apples with 200 g (7 oz) blackberries and 175 g (6 oz) demerara sugar. For the crumble topping, rub 250 g (8 oz) butter into 250 g (8 oz) plain flour in a large bowl until it resembles breadcrumbs. Mix in 125 g (4 oz) muesli and 50 g (2 oz) soft brown sugar and stir. Scatter the crumble topping evenly over the fruit. Bake in a preheated oven, 200°C (400°F), Gas Mark 6, for 20 minutes or until the fruit is cooked and bubbling juices seep through the topping. Cool for a few minutes and serve with custard.

# blackberry crumble

Serves **4**
Preparation time **10 minutes**
Cooking time **20-25 minutes**

750 g (1½ lb) **blackberries**
2 **oranges**, segmented
zest and juice of **1 orange**
**cream**, **ice cream** or **custard**,
  to serve (optional)

**Crumble topping**
200 g (7 oz) **butter**
200 g (7 oz) **plain flour**
100 g (3½ oz) **soft brown
  sugar**

**Mix** the blackberries, orange segments and the orange zest and juice together in a bowl.

**In** a separate bowl, make the crumble topping. Rub together the butter and flour with your fingertips until it resembles breadcrumbs, then stir in the sugar.

**Tip** the blackberry mixture into a large pie dish and scatter over the crumble mixture to cover.

**Bake** in a preheated oven, 220°C (425°F), Gas Mark 7, for 20–25 minutes until golden. Remove from the oven and serve warm in 4 dessert bowls with cream, ice cream or custard, if liked.

**For blackberry, orange & custard pots**, Divide 300 ml (½ pint) fresh custard among 4 dessert glasses. Whizz 200 g (7 oz) blackberries in a blender with 50 g (2 oz) caster sugar until smooth and spoon over the custard in the glasses. Peel and segment 2 large oranges and layer on top of the blackberry purée. Top each glass with a small scoop of vanilla ice cream and serve.

# index

# glossary

| UK | US |
|---|---|
| aubergine | eggplant |
| baking paper | parchment paper |
| beans, black-eyed | peas, black-eyed |
| beans, butter | beans, lima |
| biscuits | cookies |
| chilli flakes | crushed red pepper flakes |
| chopping board | cutting board |
| clingfilm | plastic wrap |
| coconut, desiccated | coconut, dry unsweetened |
| coriander | cilantro |
| cornflour | cornstarch |
| courgette | zucchini |
| couscous, giant | couscous, Israeli or pearl |
| cream, double | cream, heavy |
| flaked (nuts) | slivered (nuts) |
| flour, plain | flour, all-purpose |
| flour, self-raising | use all-purpose flour plus 1 tsp. baking powder per 125 g of flour |
| griddle pan, ridged | grill pan, ridged |
| grill | broil/broiler |
| groundnut oil | peanut oil |
| kitchen paper | paper towels |
| milk, full-fat | milk, whole |
| mushrooms, chestnut | mushrooms, cremini |
| oats, porridge | oats, rolled |

| UK | US |
|---|---|
| pak choi | bok choy |
| passata | tomato puree or sauce |
| pips | seeds |
| polenta | cornmeal |
| potatoes, King Edward /Maris Piper | potatoes, Yukon Gold |
| pulses | legumes (beans) |
| rocket | arugula |
| soft cheese | cream cheese |
| spring onions | scallions |
| stick blender | immersion blender |
| stone (avocado/peach) | pit (avocado/peach) |
| sugar, caster | sugar, superfine |
| sugar, icing | sugar, confectioners' |
| sultanas | golden raisins |
| Sunblush tomatoes | semi-dried tomatoes |
| tea towel | dish towel |
| tomato purée | tomato paste |
| vine leaves | grape leaves |
| wholemeal bread | whole-wheat bread |
| yogurt, natural | yogurt, plain |

# acknowledgements

**Editorial Director:** Natalie Bradley
**Editorial Assistant:** Constance Lam
**Proofreader:** Theresa Bebbington
**Creative Director:** Jonathan Christie
**Typesetter:** Jeremy Tilston
**Photographer:** William Heap
**Other Photography:** Stephen Conroy 28, 194; Bill Reavell 18, 56
**Food Stylists:** Sunil Vijayakar, Denise Smart, Emma Jane Frost
**Prop Stylist:** Isabel De Cordova
**Production Controllers:** Lucy Carter & Nic Jones